A
CENTENARY
SELECTION
FROM
ROBERT BROWNING'S
POETRY

A
CENTENARY
SELECTION
FROM
ROBERT BROWNING'S
POETRY

EDITED AND INTRODUCED BY
MICHAEL MEREDITH

The Browning Institute
and
Constable · London

First Published 1989

Direct correspondence concerning this work to:

In the United States	*In the United Kingdom*
The Browning Institute, Inc.	Constable & Company Limited
Box 2983, Grand Central Station	10 Orange Street
New York, NY 10163-2983	London WC2H 7EG

Library of Congress Cataloging-in-Publication Data

Browning, Robert, 1812–1889

[Poems. Selections]

A centenary selection from Robert Browning's poetry / edited and introduced by Michael Meredith.

   p.   cm.

ISBN 0-930252-25-X

ISBN 0-930252-26-8 pbk

I.   Meredith, Michael.   II.   Title.

PR4203.M47   1989

821'.8—dc20   89-34659

British Library Cataloguing in Publication Data

Browning, Robert, *1812–1889*.

A centenary selection from Robert Browning's poetry.

I.   Title   II.   Meredith, Michael

821'.8

ISBN 0-09-469390-0

ISBN 0-09-469410-9 pbk

Manufactured in the United States of America.

CONTENTS

ILLUSTRATIONS

PREFACE

THIS SELECTION FROM Robert Browning's shorter poems commemorates the one-hundredth anniversary of his death. The richness and variety of his work makes the task of choosing a mere handful of poems particularly challenging, and I am most grateful to my friends in the Browning Society and the Browning Institute for their help and encouragement. From first to last it has been a combined Anglo-American venture.

For copy-text I have followed current practice and adopted the 1889 corrected reprint of Browning's *Poetical Works* (Smith, Elder 1888–89), except for poems from *Asolando*, for which I have used the first edition. The illustrations come from many sources, but I am indebted to the Armstrong Browning Library of Baylor University for providing a substantial number from its unrivalled collection.

Mairi Calcraft has given me generous help on points of interpretation and detail, which Roy Bolton has throughout been a source of enthusiasm, wisdom and common-sense. Others who have helped in the production of this selection include Elaine Baly, Roger Brooks, Reginald Browning, Simon Calne, Betty A. Coley, Norman Collings, Edward Hagan, Pauline Hanson, Nicholas Hitchcock, Rita S. Humphrey, Joshua Latner, Scott Lewis, Edward R. Moulton-Barrett, Thomas K. Myer, Anelle O'Neil, David Plumtree, Giles Waterfield and Rosella Zorzi. To all I am most grateful.

Without Ben Glazebrook's confident support the selection would not have appeared in England. In America Philip Kelley

has characteristically given much time and valuable advice at
each stage of production. Robert Browning has no greater
champion today than Philip Kelley. Like so many recent
books on the Brownings, this selection is the better for his
interest.

INTRODUCTION

ONE HUNDRED YEARS ago Robert Browning died in his son's Venetian palazzo. With great ceremony his body was taken back to England and buried in Poets' Corner, Westminster Abbey. Fame and recognition had come late to Browning. Twenty years earlier he would have been surprised by such an official acknowledgement of his gifts. In 1868, frustrated by poor sales and obtuse criticism, he addressed the British public with good humour as "Ye who like me not." He was—and still is—one of the great unread poets of the English language.

The first aim of this centenary anthology, therefore, is to show that Browning is readable, that his poetry is accessible to that fickle English-speaking public which has claimed for over 150 years that his works are difficult to understand. Browning always defended himself from the charge of obscurity by saying that his poems were not intended as a substitute for a cigar or for a drink after dinner. His readers shouldn't expect facile truths or tinkling verse. They must be prepared to engage minds and meet the poet half-way. Browning's poems are full of talk and talkers, of pleading and pleaders. He expects a response, as his speakers challenge conventional attitudes or propose unusual strategies. One has to be alert to enjoy Browning. His poems are not difficult, although they may at times be uncomfortable.

The second purpose of the anthology is to show Browning's relevance to the late twentieth century. The belated enthusiasm for his work in the last decade of his life almost proved his undoing. By stressing Browning's morality his contemporaries directed attention the wrong way, which resulted in further public neglect during the next century.

To the late Victorians Browning was pre-eminently a teacher, a moral guide. The meaning of his poems was discussed and dissected by English and American Browning Societies, while the poet himself wryly endured a barrage of questions wherever he went. Everyone was concerned with extracting the last drop of "truth" from his poetry. Soon after his death trim little volumes appeared, bearing titles like *Guidance from Robert Browning in Matters of Faith*, or *The Ethics of Browning's Poems*. Browning became known more as a preacher than a poet. His supposed optimism was usually stressed. Pippa's claim that "God's in his Heaven, All's right with the World" became wrongly attributed to Browning himself. The guns of the First World War effectively destroyed this approach to his poetry for ever.

Neglected by the public, Browning's true value was recognized by other English poets. Thomas Hardy was the first to appreciate Browning's experiments in colloquial diction and rhyme. T.S. Eliot and Ezra Pound were interested in the dramatic monologue, the form Browning had made peculiarly his own. A post-Freudian age valued the psychological insights and opportunities the dramatic monologue provided. Contemporary poets like Richard Howard and Anthony Thwaite use monologues themselves; other poets acknowledge Browning's influence in less obvious ways. No other Victorian poet has had such a pervasive influence on the succeeding century as Browning.

Today the appeal of Browning's poetry lies in its ambiguities, its questioning, its relativism. He is no longer seen as the propounder of great truths—theologically he has little original to say—but as a poet who is himself searching for those truths. His method of inquiry, often through the use of different speakers or personae, is now appreciated as more subtle and complex than was once thought. His diction, formerly condemned as barbaric, is now recognized as years ahead of its time. Even the grotesque element in his poetry, so roundly condemned by his contemporaries, can now be seen in better perspective when the literature of the absurd is familiar to all.

In making this selection I have divided Browning's work into four convenient sections: narrative poems, love poems, dramatic monologues and personal poems. The poems within each category are arranged in a careful thematic order and are placed in increasing order of complexity. From this structure it should be possible to understand many of Browning's chief interests, and to see how different poems inter-relate and reflect each other. Each section has a short introduction, and there are explanatory and interpretative notes at the back of the book. Browning's vocabulary was twice as large as Shakespeare's, and he is among the most scholarly of poets. The notes are, therefore, intended to remove superficial difficulties and to enable the reader quickly to come to terms with each poem.

The illustrations have a similar purpose. They supplement and enrich the text in a number of ways. Some reproduce works of art which Browning describes or recreates in his poems. Others are topographical. Browning possessed a strong visual sense and conjured up in his work the sights and atmosphere of places he knew well. His poetry also provided a stimulus for contemporary painters. A few of their interpretations are included, as well as the work of later artists. Relevant photographs of Browning and of his family are also presented.

The details of Browning's life and their relationship to his poetry have been left to the end of the book. He always insisted that there was little autobiographical significance to his poetry. He claimed that he made men and women speak, and that he didn't use his own voice until the end of his life. Modern scholarship would disagree. However many masks and costumes he adopts, Browning never completely disguises his own viewpoint. The summary of his life which concludes the book attempts to relate the events of Browning's life to the poems in the anthology.

This selection is intended for those who already know some of Browning's poetry, as well as for those who are reading him for the first time. It is for this reason that I have deliberately chosen some familiar and popular poems, in addition to some that are little known. In this way I hope to give new readers an insight into the best of Browning's verse, and also to provide a fresh perspective for those already acquainted with his poems.

Yours very truly,
Robert Browning.

Robert Browning Aged About 25

Robert Browning, Senior

NARRATIVE POEMS

FROM HIS BOYHOOD Browning loved stories. The leather-bound folios in his father's library yielded him hundreds of tales from history, myth and folk-lore, many of which stayed with him during the next fifty years. Throughout his life he was a great raconteur, exchanging stories with his friends. Always he had a taste for the unusual, the dramatic and the macabre.

His simplest narrative poems are dramatically conceived with a strong theatrical flavour to them. The two tales of heroism, "Incident of the French Camp" and "How they brought the Good News" are made the more vivid by having the narrator as participant in the action. Very seldom does Browning tell his own stories; his use of an imaginary narrator often adds a fresh dimension to a poem. We have to decide when a narrator points a moral whether it is the poet's own conclusion, or whether Browning is indirectly questioning his speaker's opinion.

Browning uses some of his stories to explore less attractive aspects of human behaviour, as can be seen in "Halbert and Hob" and "The Pope and the Net." When faced with human greed and weakness, he is tolerant and sympathetic. "Apparent Failure" and "Gold Hair" show this—and at the same time demonstrate Browning's interest in the macabre. The grim realistic detail of these poems is never gratuitous; Browning's handling of the corpses in the first is as sensitive as it is startling in the second.

Browning's most ambitious narratives involve and chal-
lenge the reader. Their plots present a moral dilemma or their
conclusions are deliberately controversial, so that the reader is
drawn into a debate in which he is compelled to judge a
situation for himself. The unconventional ending to "The
Statue and the Bust" which appears to condone adultery, and
the trial at the end of "Ivàn Ivànovitch" which appears to
sanction murder, both question conventional attitudes.

There is some uneasiness in both poems. A different kind of
uneasiness characterizes "Pan and Luna." Ostensibly a retell-
ing of a legend used by Virgil in *The Georgics*, the virtuosity of
the narration, with its sensuous and erotic language, seems
deliberately to defeat the story it is trying to tell. This very
modern poem extends well beyond the scope of the conven-
tional narrative into a surrealistic dream-world. Its strange
subject, however, demonstrates the sensational and colourful
plots Browning so often chooses. Its rich telling emphasizes
the wide range of narrative styles Browning uses, and the
many varied verse forms he employs to tell a simple story.

INCIDENT OF THE FRENCH CAMP.

I.

You know, we French stormed Ratisbon:
    A mile or so away,
On a little mound, Napoleon
    Stood on our storming-day;
With neck out-thrust, you fancy how,
    Legs wide, arms locked behind,
As if to balance the prone brow
    Oppressive with its mind.

II.

Just as perhaps he mused "My plans
    "That soar, to earth may fall,
"Let once my army-leader Lannes
    "Waver at yonder wall,"—
Out 'twixt the battery-smokes there flew
    A rider, bound on bound
Full-galloping; nor bridle drew
    Until he reached the mound.

III.

Then off there flung in smiling joy,
    And held himself erect
By just his horse's mane, a boy:
    You hardly could suspect—
(So tight he kept his lips compressed,
    Scarce any blood came through)

You looked twice ere you saw his breast
  Was all but shot in two.

IV.

"Well," cried he, "Emperor, by God's grace
  "We've got you Ratisbon!
"The Marshal's in the market-place,
  "And you'll be there anon
"To see your flag-bird flap his vans
  "Where I, to heart's desire,   30
"Perched him!" The chief's eye flashed; his plans
  Soared up again like fire.

V.

The chief's eye flashed; but presently
  Softened itself, as sheathes
A film the mother-eagle's eye
  When her bruised eaglet breathes;
"You're wounded!" "Nay," the soldier's pride
  Touched to the quick, he said:
"I'm killed, Sire!" And his chief beside
  Smiling the boy fell dead.   40

"HOW THEY BROUGHT THE GOOD NEWS FROM GHENT TO AIX."

[16 — .]

I.

I SPRANG to the stirrup, and Joris, and he;
I galloped, Dirck galloped, we galloped all three;
"Good speed!" cried the watch, as the gate-bolts undrew;
"Speed!" echoed the wall to us galloping through;
Behind shut the postern, the lights sank to rest,
And into the midnight we galloped abreast.

II.

Not a word to each other; we kept the great pace
Neck by neck, stride by stride, never changing our place;
I turned in my saddle and made its girths tight,
Then shortened each stirrup, and set the pique right,   10
Rebuckled the cheek-strap, chained slacker the bit,
Nor galloped less steadily Roland a whit.

III.

'T was moonset at starting; but while we drew near
Lokeren, the cocks crew and twilight dawned clear;
At Boom, a great yellow star came out to see;
At Düffeld, 't was morning as plain as could be;
And from Mecheln church-steeple we heard the half-
    chime,
So, Joris broke silence with, "Yet there is time!"

IV.

At Aershot, up leaped of a sudden the sun,
And against him the cattle stood black every one,   20
To stare thro' the mist at us galloping past,
And I saw my stout galloper Roland at last,
With resolute shoulders, each butting away
The haze, as some bluff river headland its spray:

V.

And his low head and crest, just one sharp ear bent back
For my voice, and the other pricked out on his track;
And one eye's black intelligence, — ever that glance
O'er its white edge at me, his own master, askance!
And the thick heavy spume-flakes which aye and anon
His fierce lips shook upwards in galloping on.   30

VI.

By Hasselt, Dirck groaned; and cried Joris, "Stay spur!
"Your Roos galloped bravely, the fault's not in her,
"We'll remember at Aix"—for one heard the quick
          wheeze
Of her chest, saw the stretched neck and staggering
          knees,
And sunk tail, and horrible heave of the flank,
As down on her haunches she shuddered and sank.

VII.

So, we were left galloping, Joris and I,
Past Looz and past Tongres, no cloud in the sky;
The broad sun above laughed a pitiless laugh,
'Neath our feet broke the brittle bright stubble like
          chaff;   40

Till over by Dalhem a dome-spire sprang white,
And "Gallop," gasped Joris, "for Aix is in sight!"

VIII.

"How they'll greet us!"—and all in a moment his roan
Rolled neck and croup over, lay dead as a stone;
And there was my Roland to bear the whole weight
Of the news which alone could save Aix from her fate,
With his nostrils like pits full of blood to the brim,
And with circles of red for his eye-sockets' rim.

IX.

Then I cast loose my buffcoat, each holster let fall,
Shook off both my jack-boots, let go belt and all,   50
Stood up in the stirrup, leaned, patted his ear,
Called my Roland his pet-name, my horse without peer;
Clapped my hands, laughed and sang, any noise, bad or
        good,
Till at length into Aix Roland galloped and stood.

X.

And all I remember is—friends flocking round
As I sat with his head 'twixt my knees on the ground;
And no voice but was praising this Roland of mine,
As I poured down his throat our last measure of wine,
Which (the burgesses voted by common consent)
Was no more than his due who brought good news from
        Ghent.   60

HALBERT AND HOB.

HERE is a thing that happened. Like wild beasts whelped,
    for den,
In a wild part of North England, there lived once two
    wild men
Inhabiting one homestead, neither a hovel nor hut,
Time out of mind their birthright: father and son, these
    —but—
Such a son, such a father! Most wildness by degrees
Softens away: yet, last of their line, the wildest and worst
    were these.

Criminals, then? Why, no: they did not murder and rob;
But, give them a word, they returned a blow—old Hal-
    bert as young Hob:
Harsh and fierce of word, rough and savage of deed,
Hated or feared the more—who knows?—the genuine
    wild-beast breed.   10

Thus were they found by the few sparse folk of the
    country-side;
But how fared each with other? E'en beasts couch, hide
    by hide,
In a growling, grudged agreement: so, father and son
    aye curled
The closelier up in their den because the last of their kind
    in the world.

Still, beast irks beast on occasion. One Christmas night
    of snow,
Came father and son to words—such words! more cruel
    because the blow

To crown each word was wanting, while taunt matched
      gibe, and curse
Competed with oath in wager, like pastime in hell, —nay,
      worse:
For pastime turned to earnest, as up there sprang at last
The son at the throat of the father, seized him and held
      him fast.   20

"Out of this house you go!"—(there followed a hideous
      oath)—
"This oven where now we bake, too hot to hold us both!
If there's snow outside, there's coolness: out with you,
      bide a spell
In the drift and save the sexton the charge of a parish
      shell!"

Now, the old trunk was tough, was solid as stump of oak
Untouched at the core by a thousand years: much less had
      its seventy broke
One whipcord nerve in the muscly mass from neck to
      shoulder-blade
Of the mountainous man, whereon his child's rash hand
      like a feather weighed.

Nevertheless at once did the mammoth shut his eyes,
Drop chin to breast, drop hands to sides, stand stiffened
      —arms and thighs   30
All a piece—struck mute, much as a sentry stands,
Patient to take the enemy's fire: his captain so commands.

Whereat the son's wrath flew to fury at such sheer scorn
Of his puny strength by the giant eld thus acting the babe
      new-born:
And "Neither will this turn serve!" yelled he. "Out with
      you! Trundle, log!
If you cannot tramp and trudge like a man, try all-fours like
      a dog!"

Still the old man stood mute. So, logwise, —down to floor
Pulled from his fireside place, dragged on from hearth to
    door, —
Was he pushed, a very log, staircase along, until
A certain turn in the steps was reached, a yard from the
    house-door-sill.   40

Then the father opened eyes—each spark of their rage
    extinct, —
Temples, late black, dead-blanched, —right-hand with
    left-hand linked, —
He faced his son submissive; when slow the accents came,
They were strangely mild though his son's rash hand on
    his neck lay all the same.

"Hob, on just such a night of a Christmas long ago,
For such a cause, with such a gesture, did I drag—so—
My father down thus far: but, softening here, I heard
A voice in my heart, and stopped: you wait for an outer
    word.

"For your own sake, not mine, soften you too! Untrod
Leave this last step we reach, nor brave the finger of
    God!   50
I dared not pass its lifting: I did well. I nor blame
Nor praise you. I stopped here: and, Hob, do you the
    same!"

Straightway the son relaxed his hold of the father's throat.
They mounted, side by side, to the room again: no note
Took either of each, no sign made each to either: last
As first, in absolute silence, their Christmas-night they
    passed.

At dawn, the father sate on, dead, in the self-same place,
With an outburst blackening still the old bad fighting-face:

But the son crouched all a-tremble like any lamb new-
　　yeaned.

When he went to the burial, someone's staff he borrowed
　　—tottered and leaned.　　　　　　　　　　　　　60
But his lips were loose, not locked, —kept muttering,
　　mumbling. "There!
At his cursing and swearing!" the youngsters cried: but the
　　elders thought "In prayer."
A boy threw stones: he picked them up and stored them in
　　his vest.

So tottered, muttered, mumbled he, till he died, perhaps
　　found rest.
"Is there a reason in nature for these hard hearts?" O Lear,
That a reason out of nature must turn them soft, seems
　　clear!

THE POPE AND THE NET.

WHAT, he on whom our voices unanimously ran,
Made Pope at our last Conclave? Full low his life began:
His father earned the daily bread as just a fisherman.

So much the more his boy minds book, gives proof of
　　mother-wit,
Becomes first Deacon, and then Priest, then Bishop: see
　　him sit
No less than Cardinal ere long, while no one cries
　　"Unfit!"

But someone smirks, some other smiles, jogs elbow
　　and nods head:
Each winks at each: "'I-faith, a rise! Saint Peter's net,
　　instead

Of sword and keys, is come in vogue!" You think he
    blushes red?

Not he, of humble holy heart! "Unworthy me!" he
    sighs: 10
"From fisher's drudge to Church's prince—it is indeed
    a rise:
So, here's my way to keep the fact for ever in my eyes!"

And straightway in his palace-hall, where commonly
    is set
Some coat-of-arms, some portraiture ancestral, lo, we
    met
His mean estate's reminder in his fisher-father's net!

Which step conciliates all and some, stops cavil in a
    trice:
"The humble holy heart that holds of new-born pride
    no spice!
He's just the saint to choose for Pope!" Each adds "'T is
    my advice."

So, Pope he was: and when we flocked—its sacred
    slipper on—
To kiss his foot, we lifted eyes, alack the thing was
    gone—   20
That guarantee of lowlihead,—eclipsed that star which
    shone!

Each eyed his fellow, one and all kept silence. I cried
    "Pish!
I'll make me spokesman for the rest, express the
    common wish.
Why, Father, is the net removed?" "Son, it hath caught
    the fish."

The Old Paris Morgue

Interior of the Paris Morgue, ca. 1845

APPARENT FAILURE.

"We shall soon lose a celebrated building."
                                    Paris Newspaper.

I.

No, for I'll save it! Seven years since,
    I passed through Paris, stopped a day
To see the baptism of your Prince;
    Saw, made my bow, and went my way:
Walking the heat and headache off,
    I took the Seine-side, you surmise,
Thought of the Congress, Gortschakoff,
    Cavour's appeal and Buol's replies,
So sauntered till—what met my eyes?

II.

Only the Doric little Morgue!   10
    The dead-house where you show your drowned:
Petrarch's Vaucluse makes proud the Sorgue,
    Your Morgue has made the Seine renowned.
One pays one's debt in such a case;
    I plucked up heart and entered,—stalked,
Keeping a tolerable face
    Compared with some whose cheeks were chalked:
Let them! No Briton's to be baulked!

III.

First came the silent gazers; next,
    A screen of glass, we're thankful for;   20

Last, the sight's self, the sermon's text,
    The three men who did most abhor
Their life in Paris yesterday,
    So killed themselves: and now, enthroned
Each on his copper couch, they lay
    Fronting me, waiting to be owned.
I thought, and think, their sin's atoned.

IV.

Poor men, God made, and all for that!
    The reverence struck me; o'er each head
Religiously was hung its hat,   30
    Each coat dripped by the owner's bed,
Sacred from touch: each had his berth,
    His bounds, his proper place of rest,
Who last night tenanted on earth
    Some arch, where twelve such slept abreast, —
Unless the plain asphalte seemed best.

V.

How did it happen, my poor boy?
    You wanted to be Buonaparte
And have the Tuileries for toy,
    And could not, so it broke your heart?   40
You, old one by his side, I judge,
    Were, red as blood, a socialist,
A leveller! Does the Empire grudge
    You've gained what no Republic missed?
Be quiet, and unclench your fist!

VI.

And this — why, he was red in vain,
    Or black, — poor fellow that is blue!

What fancy was it turned your brain?
  Oh, women were the prize for you!
Money gets women, cards and dice   50
  Get money, and ill-luck gets just
The copper couch and one clear nice
  Cool squirt of water o'er your bust,
The right thing to extinguish lust!

VII.

It's wiser being good than bad;
  It's safer being meek than fierce:
It's fitter being sane than mad.
  My own hope is, a sun will pierce
The thickest cloud earth ever stretched;
  That, after Last, returns the First,   60
Though a wide compass round be fetched;
  That what began best, can't end worst,
Nor what God blessed once, prove accurst.

GOLD HAIR:

A STORY OF PORNIC.

I.

OH, the beautiful girl, too white,
  Who lived at Pornic, down by the sea,
Just where the sea and the Loire unite!
  And a boasted name in Brittany
She bore, which I will not write.

II.

Too white, for the flower of life is red;
  Her flesh was the soft seraphic screen

Of a soul that is meant (her parents said)
  To just see earth, and hardly be seen,
And blossom in heaven instead.   10

III.

Yet earth saw one thing, one how fair!
  One grace that grew to its full on earth:
Smiles might be sparse on her cheek so spare,
  And her waist want half a girdle's girth,
But she had her great gold hair.

IV.

Hair, such a wonder of flix and floss,
  Freshness and fragrance—floods of it, too!
Gold, did I say? Nay, gold's mere dross:
  Here, Life smiled, "Think what I meant to do!"
And Love sighed, "Fancy my loss!"   20

V.

So, when she died, it was scarce more strange
  Than that, when delicate evening dies,
And you follow its spent sun's pallid range,
  There's a shoot of colour startles the skies
With sudden, violent change, —

VI.

That, while the breath was nearly to seek,
  As they put the little cross to her lips,
She changed; a spot came out on her cheek,
  A spark from her eye in mid-eclipse,
And she broke forth, "I must speak!"   30

VII.

"Not my hair!" made the girl her moan—
    "All the rest is gone or to go;
"But the last, last grace, my all, my own,
    "Let it stay in the grave, that the ghosts may
        know!
"Leave my poor gold hair alone!"

VIII.

The passion thus vented, dead lay she;
    Her parents sobbed their worst on that;
All friends joined in, nor observed degree:
    For indeed the hair was to wonder at,
As it spread—not flowing free,   40

IX.

But curled around her brow, like a crown,
    And coiled beside her cheeks, like a cap,
And calmed about her neck—ay, down
    To her breast, pressed flat, without a gap
I' the gold, it reached her gown.

X.

All kissed that face, like a silver wedge
    Mid the yellow wealth, nor disturbed its hair:
E'en the priest allowed death's privilege,
    As he planted the crucifix with care
On her breast, 'twixt edge and edge.   50

XI.

And thus was she buried, inviolate
    Of body and soul, in the very space

By the altar; keeping saintly state
   In Pornic church, for her pride of race,
Pure life and piteous fate.

XII.

And in after-time would your fresh tear fall,
   Though your mouth might twitch with a
      dubious smile,
As they told you of gold, both robe and pall,
   How she prayed them leave it alone awhile,
So it never was touched at all.   60

XIII.

Years flew; this legend grew at last
   The life of the lady; all she had done,
All been, in the memories fading fast
   Of lover and friend, was summed in one
Sentence survivors passed:

XIV.

To wit, she was meant for heaven, not earth;
   Had turned an angel before the time:
Yet, since she was mortal, in such dearth
   Of frailty, all you could count a crime
Was—she knew her gold hair's worth.   70

———————————

XV.

At little pleasant Pornic church,
   It chanced, the pavement wanted repair,
Was taken to pieces: left in the lurch,

A certain sacred space lay bare,
And the boys began research.

XVI.

'T was the space where our sires would lay a saint,
    A benefactor, —a bishop, suppose,
A baron with armour-adornments quaint,
    Dame with chased ring and jewelled rose,
Things sanctity saves from taint;   80

XVII.

So we come to find them in after-days
    When the corpse is presumed to have done with
        gauds
Of use to the living, in many ways:
    For the boys get pelf, and the town applauds,
And the church deserves the praise.

XVIII.

They grubbed with a will: and at length—O *cor*
    Humanum, pectora cœca, and the rest!—
They found—no gaud they were prying for,
    No ring, no rose, but—who would have guessed?—
A double Louis-d'or!   90

XIX.

Here was a case for the priest: he heard,
    Marked, inwardly digested, laid
Finger on nose, smiled, "There's a bird
    "Chirps in my ear": then, "Bring a spade,
Dig deeper!"—he gave the word.

XX.

And lo, when they came to the coffin-lid,
   Or rotten planks which composed it once,
Why, there lay the girl's skull wedged amid
   A mint of money, it served for the nonce
To hold in its hair-heaps hid!   100

XXI.

Hid there? Why? Could the girl be wont
   (She the stainless soul) to treasure up
Money, earth's trash and heaven's affront?
   Had a spider found out the communion-cup,
Was a toad in the christening-font?

XXII.

Truth is truth: too true it was.
   Gold! She hoarded and hugged it first,
Longed for it, leaned o'er it, loved it — alas —
   Till the humour grew to a head and burst,
And she cried, at the final pass, —   110

XXIII.

"Talk not of God, my heart is stone!
   "Nor lover nor friend — be gold for both!
"Gold I lack; and, my all, my own,
   "It shall hide in my hair. I scarce die loth
"If they let my hair alone!"

XXIV.

Louis-d'or, some six times five,
   And duly double, every piece.
Now do you see? With the priest to shrive,

With parents preventing her soul's release
By kisses that kept alive, —   120

XXV.

With heaven's gold gates about to ope,
  With friends' praise, gold-like, lingering still,
An instinct had bidden the girl's hand grope
    For gold, the true sort—"Gold in heaven,
        if you will;
"But I keep earth's too, I hope."

XXVI.

Enough! The priest took the grave's grim yield:
  The parents, they eyed that price of sin
As if *thirty pieces* lay revealed
    On the place *to bury strangers in*,
The hideous Potter's Field.   130

XXVII.

But the priest bethought him: "'Milk that's spilt'
  "—You know the adage! Watch and pray!
"Saints tumble to earth with so slight a tilt!
    "It would build a new altar; that, we may!"
And the altar therewith was built.

XXVIII.

Why I deliver this horrible verse?
  As the text of a sermon, which now I preach:
Evil or good may be better or worse
  In the human heart, but the mixture of each
Is a marvel and a curse.   140

XXIX.

The candid incline to surmise of late
   That the Christian faith proves false, I find:
For our Essays-and-Reviews' debate
   Begins to tell on the public mind,
And Colenso's words have weight:

XXX.

I still, to suppose it true, for my part,
   See reasons and reasons; this, to begin:
'T is the faith that launched point-blank her dart
   At the head of a lie — taught Original Sin,
The Corruption of Man's Heart.   150

THE STATUE AND THE BUST.

THERE'S a palace in Florence, the world knows well,
And a statue watches it from the square,
And this story of both do our townsmen tell.

Ages ago, a lady there,
At the farthest window facing the East
Asked, "Who rides by with the royal air?"

The bridesmaids' prattle around her ceased;
She leaned forth, one on either hand;
They saw how the blush of the bride increased —

They felt by its beats her heart expand —   10
As one at each ear and both in a breath
Whispered, "The Great-Duke Ferdinand."

That self-same instant, underneath,
The Duke rode past in his idle way,
Empty and fine like a swordless sheath.

Gay he rode, with a friend as gay,
Till he threw his head back—"Who is she?"
—"A bride the Riccardi brings home to-day."

Hair in heaps lay heavily
Over a pale brow spirit-pure—   20
Carved like the heart of the coal-black tree,

Crisped like a war-steed's encolure—
And vainly sought to dissemble her eyes
Of the blackest black our eyes endure.

And lo, a blade for a knight's emprise
Filled the fine empty sheath of a man,—
The Duke grew straightway brave and wise.

He looked at her, as a lover can;
She looked at him, as one who awakes:
The past was a sleep, and her life began.   30

Now, love so ordered for both their sakes,
A feast was held that selfsame night
In the pile which the mighty shadow makes.

(For Via Larga is three-parts light,
But the palace overshadows one,
Because of a crime which may God requite!

To Florence and God the wrong was done,
Through the first republic's murder there
By Cosimo and his cursed son.)

The Duke (with the statue's face in the square)   40
Turned in the midst of his multitude
At the bright approach of the bridal pair.

Face to face the lovers stood
A single minute and no more,
While the bridegroom bent as a man subdued—

Bowed till his bonnet brushed the floor—
For the Duke on the lady a kiss conferred,
As the courtly custom was of yore.

In a minute can lovers exchange a word?
If a word did pass, which I do not think,   50
Only one out of the thousand heard.

That was the bridegroom. At day's brink
He and his bride were alone at last
In a bedchamber by a taper's blink.

Calmly he said that her lot was cast,
That the door she had passed was shut on her
Till the final catafalk repassed.

The world meanwhile, its noise and stir,
Through a certain window facing the East,
She could watch like a convent's chronicler.   60

Since passing the door might lead to a feast,
And a feast might lead to so much beside,
He, of many evils, chose the least.

"Freely I choose too," said the bride—
"Your window and its world suffice,"
Replied the tongue, while the heart replied—

"If I spend the night with that devil twice,
"May his window serve as my loop of hell
"Whence a damned soul looks on paradise!

"I fly to the Duke who loves me well,   70
"Sit by his side and laugh at sorrow
"Ere I count another ave-bell.

"'T is only the coat of a page to borrow,
"And tie my hair in a horse-boy's trim,
"And I save my soul—but not to-morrow"—

(She checked herself and her eye grew dim)
"My father tarries to bless my state:
"I must keep it one day more for him.

"Is one day more so long to wait?
"Moreover the Duke rides past, I know;   80
"We shall see each other, sure as fate."

She turned on her side and slept. Just so!
So we resolve on a thing and sleep:
So did the lady, ages ago.

That night the Duke said, "Dear or cheap
"As the cost of this cup of bliss may prove
"To body or soul, I will drain it deep."

And on the morrow, bold with love,
He beckoned the bridegroom (close on call,
As his duty bade, by the Duke's alcove)   90

And smiled "'T was a very funeral,
"Your lady will think, this feast of ours,—
"A shame to efface, whate'er befall!

"What if we break from the Arno bowers,
"And try if Petraja, cool and green,
"Cure last night's fault with this morning's flowers?"

The bridegroom, not a thought to be seen
On his steady brow and quiet mouth,
Said, "Too much favour for me so mean!

"But, alas! my lady leaves the South;   100
"Each wind that comes from the Apennine
"Is a menace to her tender youth:

"Nor a way exists, the wise opine,
"If she quits her palace twice this year,
"To avert the flower of life's decline."

Quoth the Duke, "A sage and a kindly fear.
"Moreover Petraja is cold this spring:
"Be our feast to-night as usual here!"

And then to himself—"Which night shall bring
"Thy bride to her lover's embraces, fool—   110
"Or I am the fool, and thou art the king!

"Yet my passion must wait a night, nor cool—
"For to-night the Envoy arrives from France
"Whose heart I unlock with thyself, my tool.

"I need thee still and might miss perchance.
"To-day is not wholly lost, beside,
"With its hope of my lady's countenance:

"For I ride—what should I do but ride?
"And passing her palace, if I list,
"May glance at its window—well betide!"   120

So said, so done: nor the lady missed
One ray that broke from the ardent brow,
Nor a curl of the lips where the spirit kissed.

Be sure that each renewed the vow,
No morrow's sun should arise and set
And leave them then as it left them now.

But next day passed, and next day yet,
With still fresh cause to wait one day more
Ere each leaped over the parapet.

And still, as love's brief morning wore,   130
With a gentle start, half smile, half sigh,
They found love not as it seemed before.

They thought it would work infallibly,
But not in despite of heaven and earth:
The rose would blow when the storm passed by.

Meantime they could profit in winter's dearth
By store of fruits that supplant the rose:
The world and its ways have a certain worth:

And to press a point while these oppose
Were simple policy; better wait: 140
We lose no friends and we gain no foes.

Meantime, worse fates than a lover's fate,
Who daily may ride and pass and look
Where his lady watches behind the grate!

And she—she watched the square like a book
Holding one picture and only one,
Which daily to find she undertook:

When the picture was reached the book was done,
And she turned from the picture at night to scheme
Of tearing it out for herself next sun.   150

So weeks grew months, years; gleam by gleam
The glory dropped from their youth and love,
And both perceived they had dreamed a dream;

Which hovered as dreams do, still above:
But who can take a dream for a truth?
Oh, hide our eyes from the next remove!

One day as the lady saw her youth
Depart, and the silver thread that streaked
Her hair, and, worn by the serpent's tooth,

The brow so puckered, the chin so peaked, —   160
And wondered who the woman was,
Hollow-eyed and haggard-cheeked,

Fronting her silent in the glass—
"Summon here," she suddenly said,
"Before the rest of my old self pass,

"Him, the Carver, a hand to aid,
"Who fashions the clay no love will change,
"And fixes a beauty never to fade.

"Let Robbia's craft so apt and strange
"Arrest the remains of young and fair,   170
"And rivet them while the seasons range.

"Make me a face on the window there,
"Waiting as ever, mute the while,
"My love to pass below in the square!

A Della Robbia Bust

Grand–Duke Ferdinand

"And let me think that it may beguile
"Dreary days which the dead must spend
"Down in their darkness under the aisle,

"To say, 'What matters it at the end?
"'I did no more while my heart was warm
"'Than does that image, my pale-faced friend.'   180

"Where is the use of the lip's red charm,
"The heaven of hair, the pride of the brow,
"And the blood that blues the inside arm—

"Unless we turn, as the soul knows how,
"The earthly gift to an end divine?
"A lady of clay is as good, I trow."

But long ere Robbia's cornice, fine,
With flowers and fruits which leaves enlace,
Was set where now is the empty shrine—

(And, leaning out of a bright blue space,   190
As a ghost might lean from a chink of sky,
The passionate pale lady's face—

Eyeing ever, with earnest eye
And quick-turned neck at its breathless stretch,
Some one who ever is passing by—)

The Duke had sighed like the simplest wretch
In Florence, "Youth—my dream escapes!
"Will its record stay?" And he bade them fetch

Some subtle moulder of brazen shapes—
"Can the soul, the will, die out of a man   200
"Ere his body find the grave that gapes?

"John of Douay shall effect my plan,
"Set me on horseback here aloft,
"Alive, as the crafty sculptor can,

"In the very square I have crossed so oft:
"That men may admire, when future suns
"Shall touch the eyes to a purpose soft,

"While the mouth and the brow stay brave in
        bronze—
"Admire and say, 'When he was alive
"'How he would take his pleasure once!'   210

"And it shall go hard but I contrive
"To listen the while, and laugh in my tomb
"At idleness which aspires to strive."

————————

So! While these wait the trump of doom,
How do their spirits pass, I wonder,
Nights and days in the narrow room?

Still, I suppose, they sit and ponder
What a gift life was, ages ago,
Six steps out of the chapel yonder.

Only they see not God, I know,   220
Nor all that chivalry of his,
The soldier-saints who, row on row,

Burn upward each to his point of bliss—
Since, the end of life being manifest,
He had burned his way thro' the world to this.

I hear you reproach, "But delay was best,
"For their end was a crime."—Oh, a crime will do
As well, I reply, to serve for a test,

As a virtue golden through and through,
Sufficient to vindicate itself   230
And prove its worth at a moment's view!

Must a game be played for the sake of pelf?
Where a button goes, 't were an epigram
To offer the stamp of the very Guelph.

The true has no value beyond the sham:
As well the counter as coin, I submit,
When your table's a hat, and your prize a dram.

Stake your counter as boldly every whit,
Venture as warily, use the same skill,
Do your best, whether winning or losing it,   240

If you choose to play!—is my principle.
Let a man contend to the uttermost
For his life's set prize, be it what it will!

The counter our lovers staked was lost
As surely as if it were lawful coin:
And the sin I impute to each frustrate ghost

Is—the unlit lamp and the ungirt loin,
Though the end in sight was a vice, I say.
You of the virtue (we issue join)
How strive you? *De te, fabula.*   250

IVÀN IVÀNOVITCH.

"THEY tell me, your carpenters," quoth I to my friend
    the Russ,
"Make a simple hatchet serve as a tool-box serves with
    us.
Arm but each man with his axe, 't is a hammer and saw
    and plane
And chisel, and—what know I else? We should imitate
    in vain
The mastery wherewithal, by a flourish of just the adze,
He cleaves, clamps, dovetails in,—no need of our nails
    and brads,—
The manageable pine: 't is said he could shave himself
With the axe,—so all adroit, now a giant and now an elf,
Does he work and play at once!"
                       Quoth my friend the Russ to me,
"Ay, that and more beside on occasion! It scarce may
    be   10
You never heard tell a tale told children, time out of
    mind,
By father and mother and nurse, for a moral that's
    behind,
Which children quickly seize. If the incident happened
    at all,
We place it in Peter's time when hearts were great not
    small,
Germanized, Frenchified. I wager 't is old to you
As the story of Adam and Eve, and possibly quite as
    true."

In the deep of our land, 't is said, a village from out the
    woods

Emerged on the great main-road 'twixt two great soli-
    tudes.
Through forestry right and left, black verst and verst of
    pine,
From village to village runs the road's long wide bare
    line.   20
Clearance and clearance break the else-unconquered
    growth
Of pine and all that breeds and broods there, leaving
    loth
Man's inch of masterdom,—spot of life, spirt of fire,—
To star the dark and dread, lest right and rule expire
Throughout the monstrous wild, a-hungered to resume
Its ancient sway, suck back the world into its womb:
Defrauded by man's craft which clove from North to
    South
This highway broad and straight e'en from the Neva's
    mouth
To Moscow's gates of gold. So, spot of life and spirt
Of fire aforesaid, burn, each village death-begirt   30
By wall and wall of pine—unprobed undreamed abyss.

Early one winter morn, in such a village as this,
Snow-whitened everywhere except the middle road
Ice-roughed by track of sledge, there worked by his abode
Ivàn Ivànovitch, the carpenter, employed
On a huge shipmast trunk; his axe now trimmed and
    toyed
With branch and twig, and now some chop athwart the
    bole
Changed bole to billets, bared at once the sap and soul.
About him, watched the work his neighbours sheepskin-
    clad;
Each bearded mouth puffed steam, each grey eye twin-
    kled glad   40
To see the sturdy arm which, never stopping play,

Proved strong man's blood still boils, freeze winter as he
    may.

Sudden, a burst of bells. Out of the road, on edge
Of the hamlet—horse's hoofs galloping. "How, a
    sledge?
What's here?" cried all as—in, up to the open space,
Workyard and market-ground, folk's common meeting-
    place,—
Stumbled on, till he fell, in one last bound for life,
A horse: and, at his heels, a sledge held—"Dmìtri's wife!
Back without Dmìtri too! and children—where are
    they?
Only a frozen corpse!"

                  They drew it forth: then—"Nay,   50
Not dead, though like to die! Gone hence a month ago:
Home again, this rough jaunt—alone through night and
    snow—
What can the cause be? Hark—Droug, old horse, how
    he groans:
His day's done! Chafe away, keep chafing, for she
    moans:
She's coming to! Give here: see, motherkin, your
    friends!
Cheer up, all safe at home! Warm inside makes
    amends
For outside cold,—sup quick! Don't look as we were
    bears!
What is it startles you? What strange adventure stares
Up at us in your face? You know friends—which is
    which?
I'm Vàssili, he's Sergeì, Ivàn Ivànovitch . . ."   60

At the word, the woman's eyes, slow-wandering till they
    neared
The blue eyes o'er the bush of honey-coloured beard,

Took in full light and sense and—torn to rags, some
        dream
Which hid the naked truth—O loud and long the scream
She gave, as if all power of voice within her throat
Poured itself wild away to waste in one dread note!
Then followed gasps and sobs, and then the steady flow
Of kindly tears: the brain was saved, a man might know.
Down fell her face upon the good friend's propping
        knee;
His broad hands smoothed her head, as fain to brush it
        free   70
From fancies, swarms that stung like bees unhived. He
        soothed—
"Loukèria, Loùscha!"—still he, fondling, smoothed and
        smoothed.
At last her lips formed speech.

                        "Ivàn, dear—you indeed!
You, just the same dear you! While I ... O intercede,
Sweet Mother, with thy Son Almighty—let his might
Bring yesterday once more, undo all done last night!
But this time yesterday, Ivàn, I sat like you,
A child on either knee, and, dearer than the two,
A babe inside my arms, close to my heart—that's lost
In morsels o'er the snow! Father, Son, Holy Ghost,   80
Cannot you bring again my blessed yesterday?"

When no more tears would flow, she told her tale: this
        way.

"Maybe, a month ago, —was it not?—news came here,
They wanted, deeper down, good workmen fit to rear
A church and roof it in. 'We'll go,' my husband said:
'None understands like me to melt and mould their
        lead.'
So, friends here helped us off—Ivàn, dear, you the first!

How gay we jingled forth, all five—(my heart will
      burst)—
While Dmìtri shook the reins, urged Droug upon his
      track!

"Well, soon the month ran out, we just were coming
      back,   90
When yesterday—behold, the village was on fire!
Fire ran from house to house. What help, as, nigh and
      nigher,
The flames came furious? 'Haste,' cried Dmìtri, 'men
      must do
The little good man may: to sledge and in with you,
You and our three! We check the fire by laying flat
Each building in its path, —I needs must stay for that, —
But you ... no time for talk! Wrap round you every
      rug,
Cover the couple close, —you'll have the babe to hug.
No care to guide old Droug, he knows his way, by guess,
Once start him on the road: but chirrup, none the
      less!   100
The snow lies glib as glass and hard as steel, and soon
You'll have rise, fine and full, a marvel of a moon.
Hold straight up, all the same, this lighted twist of pitch!
Once home and with our friend Ivàn Ivànovitch,
All's safe: I have my pay in pouch, all's right with me,
So I but find as safe you and our precious three!
Off, Droug!'—because the flames had reached us, and
      the men
Shouted 'But lend a hand, Dmìtri—as good as ten!'

"So, in we bundled—I, and those God gave me once;
Old Droug, that's stiff at first, seemed youthful for the
      nonce: 110
He understood the case, galloping straight ahead.
Out came the moon: my twist soon dwindled, feebly red

In that unnatural day—yes, daylight, bred between
Moon-light and snow-light, lamped those grotto-depths
         which screen
Such devils from God's eye. Ah, pines, how straight you
         grow
Nor bend one pitying branch, true breed of brutal snow!
Some undergrowth had served to keep the devils blind
While we escaped outside their border!

                                      "Was that—wind?
Anyhow, Droug starts, stops, back go his ears, he snuffs,
Snorts,—never such a snort! then plunges, knows the
         sough's   120
Only the wind: yet, no—our breath goes up too
         straight!
Still the low sound,—less low, loud, louder, at a rate
There's no mistaking more! Shall I lean out—look—
         learn
The truth whatever it be? Pad, pad! At last, I turn—

"'T is the regular pad of the wolves in pursuit of
         the life in the sledge!
An army they are: close-packed they press like
         the thrust of a wedge:
They increase as they hunt: for I see, through the pine-
         trunks ranged each side,
Slip forth new fiend and fiend, make wider and still more
         wide
The four-footed steady advance. The foremost—none
         may pass:
They are elders and lead the line, eye and eye—green-
         glowing brass!
But a long way distant still. Droug, save us! He does
         his best:
Yet they gain on us, gain, till they reach,—one reaches...
         How utter the rest?

O that Satan-faced first of the band! How he lolls out
    the length of his tongue,
How he laughs and lets gleam his white teeth! He is
    on me, his paws pry among
The wraps and the rugs! O my pair, my twin-pigeons,
    lie still and seem dead!
Stepàn, he shall never have you for a meal, —here's your
    mother instead!
No, he will not be counselled—must cry, poor Stiòpka,
    so foolish! though first
Of my boy-brood, he was not the best: nay, neighbours
    have called him the worst:
He was puny, an undersized slip, —a darling to me, all
    the same!
But little there was to be praised in the boy, and a plenty
    to blame.   140
I loved him with heart and soul, yes—but, deal him a
    blow for a fault,
He would sulk for whole days. 'Foolish boy! lie still
    or the villain will vault,
Will snatch you from over my head!' No use! he cries,
    screams, —who can hold
Fast a boy in a frenzy of fear! It follows—as I foretold!
The Satan-face snatched and snapped: I tugged, I tore
    —and then
His brother too needs must shriek! If one must go, 't is
    men
The Tsar needs, so we hear, not ailing boys! Perhaps
My hands relaxed their grasp, got tangled in the wraps:
God, he was gone! I looked: there tumbled the cursed
    crew,
Each fighting for a share: too busy to pursue!   150
That's so far gain at least: Droug, gallop another verst
Or two, or three—God sends we beat them, arrive the
    first!
A mother who boasts two boys was ever accounted rich:

Some have not a boy: some have, but lose him,—God
    knows which
Is worse: how pitiful to see your weakling pine
And pale and pass away! Strong brats, this pair of mine!

"O misery! for while I settle to what near seems
Content, I am 'ware again of the tramp, and again there
    gleams—
Point and point—the line, eyes, levelled green brassy
    fire!
So soon is resumed your chase? Will nothing appease,
    nought tire   160
The furies? And yet I think—I am certain the race is
    slack,
And the numbers are nothing like. Not a quarter of
    the pack!
Feasters and those full-fed are staying behind ... Ah
    why?
We'll sorrow for that too soon! Now,—gallop, reach
    home, and die,
Nor ever again leave house, to trust our life in the trap
For life—we call a sledge! Teriòscha, in my lap!
Yes, I'll lie down upon you, tight-tie you with the
    strings
Here—of my heart! No fear, this time, your mother
    flings ...
Flings? I flung? Never! But think!—a woman, after all
Contending with a wolf! Save you I must and shall,   170
Terentiì!
             "How now? What, you still head the race,
Your eyes and tongue and teeth crave fresh food, Satan-
    face?
There and there! Plain I struck green fire out! Flash again?
All a poor fist can do to damage eyes proves vain!
My fist—why not crunch that? He is wanton for ...
    O God,

Why give this wolf his taste? Common wolves scrape
     and prod
The earth till out they scratch some corpse—mere putrid
     flesh!
Why must this glutton leave the faded, choose the
     fresh?
Terentiì—God, feel!—his neck keeps fast thy bag
Of holy things, saints' bones, this Satan-face will drag   180
Forth, and devour along with him, our Pope declared
The relics were to save from danger!

                              "Spurned, not spared!
'T was through my arms, crossed arms, he—nuzzling
     now with snout,
Now ripping, tooth and claw—plucked, pulled Terentiì
     out,
A prize indeed! I saw—how could I else but see?—
My precious one—I bit to hold back—pulled from me!
Up came the others, fell to dancing—did the imps!—
Skipped as they scampered round. There's one is grey,
     and limps:
Who knows but old bad Màrpha,—she always owed me
     spite
And envied me my births,—skulks out of doors at night   190
And turns into a wolf, and joins the sisterhood,
And laps the youthful life, then slinks from out the wood,
Squats down at door by dawn, spins there demure as erst
—No strength, old crone,—not she!—to crawl forth
     half a verst!

"Well, I escaped with one: 'twixt one and none there
     lies
The space 'twixt heaven and hell. And see, a rose-light
     dyes
The endmost snow: 't is dawn, 't is day, 't is safe at home!
We have outwitted you! Ay, monsters, snarl and foam,

Russian Woman Abandoning Her Children to the Wolves

Robert Browning Aged 56

Fight each the other fiend, disputing for a share, —
Forgetful, in your greed, our finest off we bear,   200
Tough Droug and I, — my babe, my boy that shall be
        man,
My man that shall be more, do all a hunter can
To trace and follow and find and catch and crucify
Wolves, wolfkins, all your crew! A thousand deaths
        shall die
The whimperingest cub that ever squeezed the teat!
'Take that!' we'll stab you with, — 'the tenderness we
        met
When, wretches, you danced round—not this, thank
        God—not this!
Hellhounds, we baulk you!'

                    "But—Ah, God above!—Bliss, bliss—
Not the band, no! And yet—yes, for Droug knows
        him! One—
This only of them all has said 'She saves a son!   210
His fellows disbelieve such luck: but he believes,
He lets them pick the bones, laugh at him in their sleeves:
He's off and after us, —one speck, one spot, one ball
Grows bigger, bound on bound, —one wolf as good as
        all!
Oh but I know the trick! Have at the snaky tongue!
That's the right way with wolves! Go, tell your mates
        I wrung
The panting morsel out, left you to howl your worst!
Now for it—now! Ah me! I know him—thrice-accurst
Satan-face, —him to the end my foe!

                    "All fight's in vain:
This time the green brass points pierce to my very
        brain.
                                        220
I fall—fall as I ought—quite on the babe I guard:
I overspread with flesh the whole of him. Too hard

To die this way, torn piecemeal? Move hence? Not I
    —one inch!
Gnaw through me, through and through: flat thus I lie
    nor flinch!
O God, the feel of the fang furrowing my shoulder!—
    see!
It grinds—it grates the bone. O Kìrill under me,
Could I do more? Beside he knew wolf's way to win:
I clung, closed round like wax: yet in he wedged and in,
Past my neck, past my breasts, my heart, until . . . how
    feels
The onion-bulb your knife parts, pushing through its
    peels,   230
Till out you scoop its clove wherein lie stalk and leaf
And bloom and seed unborn?

                           "That slew me: yes, in brief,
I died then, dead I lay doubtlessly till Droug stopped
Here, I suppose. I come to life, I find me propped
Thus—how or when or why,—I know not. Tell me,
    friends,
All was a dream: laugh quick and say the nightmare
    ends!
Soon I shall find my house: 't is over there: in proof,
Save for that chimney heaped with snow, you'd see the
    roof
Which holds my three—my two—my one—not one?

                           "Life's mixed
With misery, yet we live—must live. The Satan fixed   240
His face on mine so fast, I took its print as pitch
Takes what it cools beneath. Ivàn Ivànovitch,
'T is you unharden me, you thaw, disperse the thing!
Only keep looking kind, the horror will not cling.
Your face smooths fast away each print of Satan. Tears

—What good they do! Life's sweet, and all its after-
    years,
Ivàn Ivànovitch, I owe you! Yours am I!
May God reward you, dear!"

                     Down she sank. Solemnly
Ivàn rose, raised his axe,—for fitly, as she knelt,
Her head lay: well-apart, each side, her arms hung,—
    dealt   250
Lightning-swift thunder-strong one blow—no need of
    more!
Headless she knelt on still: that pine was sound at core
(Neighbours were used to say)—cast-iron-kernelled—
    which
Taxed for a second stroke Ivàn Ivànovitch.

The man was scant of words as strokes. "It had to be:
I could no other: God it was bade 'Act for me!'"
Then stooping, peering round—what is it now he lacks?
A proper strip of bark wherewith to wipe his axe.
Which done, he turns, goes in, closes the door behind.
The others mute remain, watching the blood-snake
    wind   260
Into a hiding-place among the splinter-heaps.

At length, still mute, all move: one lifts,—from where it
    steeps
Redder each ruddy rag of pine,—the head: two more
Take up the dripping body: then, mute still as before,
Move in a sort of march, march on till marching ends
Opposite to the church; where halting,—who suspends,
By its long hair, the thing, deposits in its place
The piteous head: once more the body shows no trace
Of harm done: there lies whole the Loùscha, maid and
    wife

And mother, loved until this latest of her life.   270
Then all sit on the bank of snow which bounds a space
Kept free before the porch for judgment: just the place!

Presently all the souls, man, woman, child, which make
The village up, are found assembling for the sake
Of what is to be done. The very Jews are there:
A Gipsy troop, though bound with horses for the Fair,
Squats with the rest. Each heart with its conception
          seethes
And simmers, but no tongue speaks: one may say, —
          none breathes.

Anon from out the church totters the Pope — the priest —
Hardly alive, so old, a hundred years at least.   280
With him, the Commune's head, a hoary senior too,
Stàrosta, that's his style, — like Equity Judge with
          you, —
Natural Jurisconsult: then, fenced about with furs,
Pomeschìk, — Lord of the Land, who wields — and none
          demurs —
A power of life and death. They stoop, survey the corpse.

Then, straightened on his staff, the Stàrosta — the
          thorpe's
Sagaciousest old man — hears what you just have heard,
From Droug's first inrush, all, up to Ivàn's last word
"God bade me act for him: I dared not disobey!"

Silence — the Pomeschìk broke with "A wild wrong
          way   290
Of righting wrong — if wrong there were, such wrath to
          rouse!
Why was not law observed? What article allows

Whoso may please to play the judge, and, judgment
      dealt,
Play executioner, as promptly as we pelt
To death, without appeal, the vermin whose sole fault
Has been—it dared to leave the darkness of its vault,
Intrude upon our day! Too sudden and too rash!
What was this woman's crime? Suppose the church
      should crash
Down where I stand, your lord: bound are my serfs to
      dare
Their utmost that I 'scape: yet, if the crashing scare   300
My children,—as you are,—if sons fly, one and all,
Leave father to his fate,—poor cowards though I call
The runaways, I pause before I claim their life
Because they prized it more than mine. I would each
      wife
Died for her husband's sake, each son to save his sire:
'T is glory, I applaud—scarce duty, I require.
Ivàn Ivànovitch has done a deed that's named
Murder by law and me: who doubts, may speak un-
      blamed!"

All turned to the old Pope. "Ay, children, I am old—
How old, myself have got to know no longer. Rolled   310
Quite round, my orb of life, from infancy to age,
Seems passing back again to youth. A certain stage
At least I reach, or dream I reach, where I discern
Truer truths, laws behold more lawlike than we learn
When first we set our foot to tread the course I trod
With man to guide my steps: who leads me now is God.
'Your young men shall see visions:' and in my youth I
      saw
And paid obedience to man's visionary law:
'Your old men shall dream dreams:' and, in my age, a
      hand

Conducts me through the cloud round law to where I
     stand   320
Firm on its base,—know cause, who, before, knew
     effect.

"The world lies under me: and nowhere I detect
So great a gift as this—God's own—of human life.
'Shall the dead praise thee?' No! 'The whole live world
     is rife,
God, with thy glory,' rather! Life then, God's best of
     gifts,
For what shall man exchange? For life—when so he
     shifts
The weight and turns the scale, lets life for life restore
God's balance, sacrifice the less to gain the more,
Substitute—for low life, another's or his own—
Life large and liker God's who gave it: thus alone   330
May life extinguish life that life may trulier be!
How low this law descends on earth, is not for me
To trace: complexed becomes the simple, intricate
The plain, when I pursue law's winding. 'T is the straight
Outflow of law I know and name: to law, the fount
Fresh from God's footstool, friends, follow while I
     remount.

"A mother bears a child: perfection is complete
So far in such a birth. Enabled to repeat
The miracle of life,—herself was born so just
A type of womankind, that God sees fit to trust   340
Her with the holy task of giving life in turn.
Crowned by this crowning pride,—how say you,
     should she spurn
Regality—discrowned, unchilded, by her choice
Of barrenness exchanged for fruit which made rejoice
Creation, though life's self were lost in giving birth

To life more fresh and fit to glorify God's earth?
How say you, should the hand God trusted with life's
    torch
Kindled to light the world—aware of sparks that scorch,
Let fall the same? Forsooth, her flesh a fire-flake stings
The mother drops the child! Among what monstrous
    things   350
Shall she be classed? Because of motherhood, each male
Yields to his partner place, sinks proudly in the scale:
His strength owned weakness, wit—folly, and cour-
    age—fear,
Beside the female proved male's mistress—only here.
The fox-dam, hunger-pined, will slay the felon sire
Who dares assault her whelp: the beaver, stretched on
    fire,
Will die without a groan: no pang avails to wrest
Her young from where they hide—her sanctuary breast.
What's here then? Answer me, thou dead one, as, I trow,
Standing at God's own bar, he bids thee answer now!   360
Thrice crowned was thou—each crown of pride, a child
    —thy charge!
Where are they? Lost? Enough: no need that thou
    enlarge
On how or why the loss: life left to utter 'lost'
Condemns itself beyond appeal. The soldier's post
Guards from the foe's attack the camp he sentinels:
That he no traitor proved, this and this only tells—
Over the corpse of him trod foe to foe's success.
Yet—one by one thy crowns torn from thee—thou no
    less
To scare the world, shame God, —livedst! I hold He saw
The unexampled sin, ordained the novel law,   370
Whereof first instrument was first intelligence
Found loyal here. I hold that, failing human sense,
The very earth had oped, sky fallen, to efface

Humanity's new wrong, motherhood's first disgrace.
Earth oped not, neither fell the sky, for prompt was
        found
A man and man enough, head-sober and heart-sound,
Ready to hear God's voice, resolute to obey.
Ivàn Ivànovitch, I hold, has done, this day,
No otherwise than did, in ages long ago,
Moses when he made known the purport of that flow   380
Of fire athwart the law's twain-tables! I proclaim
Ivàn Ivànovitch God's servant!"

                            At which name
Uprose that creepy whisper from out the crowd, is wont
To swell and surge and sink when fellow-men confront
A punishment that falls on fellow flesh and blood,
Appallingly beheld—shudderingly understood,
No less, to be the right, the just, the merciful.
"God's servant!" hissed the crowd.

                            When that Amen grew dull
And died away and left acquittal plain adjudged,
"Amen!" last sighed the lord. "There's none shall say
        I grudged   390
Escape from punishment in such a novel case.
Deferring to old age and holy life,—be grace
Granted! say I. No less, scruples might shake a sense
Firmer than I boast mine. Law's law, and evidence
Of breach therein lies plain,—blood-red-bright,—all
        may see!
Yet all absolve the deed: absolved the deed must be!

"And next—as mercy rules the hour—methinks 't were
        well
You signify forthwith its sentence, and dispel
The doubts and fears, I judge, which busy now the head

Law puts a halter round—a halo—you, instead!   400
Ivàn Ivànovitch—what think you he expects
Will follow from his feat? Go, tell him—law protects
Murder, for once: no need he longer keep behind
The Sacred Pictures—where skulks Innocence enshrined,
Or I missay! Go, some! You others, haste and hide
The dismal object there: get done, whate'er betide!"

So, while the youngers raised the corpse, the elders
          trooped
Silently to the house: where halting, someone stooped,
Listened beside the door; all there was silent too.
Then they held counsel; then pushed door and, passing
          through,   410
Stood in the murderer's presence.
                              Ivàn Ivànovitch
Knelt, building on the floor that Kremlin rare and rich
He deftly cut and carved on lazy winter nights.
Some five young faces watched, breathlessly, as, to
          rights,
Piece upon piece, he reared the fabric nigh complete.
Stèscha, Ivàn's old mother, sat spinning by the heat
Of the oven where his wife Kàtia stood baking bread.
Ivàn's self, as he turned his honey-coloured head,
Was just in act to drop, 'twixt fir-cones,—each a
          dome,—
The scooped-out yellow gourd presumably the home   420
Of Kolokol the Big: the bell, therein to hitch,
—An acorn-cup—was ready: Ivàn Ivànovitch
Turned with it in his mouth.

                    They told him he was free
As air to walk abroad. "How otherwise?" asked he.

PAN AND LUNA.

Si credere dignum est. — *Georgic.* iii. 390.

O WORTHY of belief I hold it was,
Virgil, your legend in those strange three lines!
No question, that adventure came to pass
One black night in Arcadia: yes, the pines,
Mountains and valleys mingling made one mass
Of black with void black heaven: the earth's con-
      fines,
The sky's embrace, —below, above, around,
All hardened into black without a bound.

Fill up a swart stone chalice to the brim
With fresh-squeezed yet fast-thickening poppy-juice: 10
See how the sluggish jelly, late a-swim,
Turns marble to the touch of who would loose
The solid smooth, grown jet from rim to rim,
By turning round the bowl! So night can fuse
Earth with her all-comprising sky. No less,
Light, the least spark, shows air and emptiness.

And thus it proved when—diving into space,
Stript of all vapour, from each web of mist
Utterly film-free—entered on her race
The naked Moon, full-orbed antagonist   20
Of night and dark, night's dowry: peak to base,
Upstarted mountains, and each valley, kissed
To sudden life, lay silver-bright: in air
Flew she revealed, Maid-Moon with limbs all bare.

Still as she fled, each depth—where refuge seemed—
Opening a lone pale chamber, left distinct

Those limbs: mid still-retreating blue, she teemed
Herself with whiteness,—virginal, uncinct
By any halo save what finely gleamed
To outline not disguise her: heaven was linked   30
In one accord with earth to quaff the joy,
Drain beauty to the dregs without alloy.

Whereof she grew aware. What help? When, lo,
A succourable cloud with sleep lay dense:
Some pine-tree-top had caught it sailing slow,
And tethered for a prize: in evidence
Captive lay fleece on fleece of piled-up snow
Drowsily patient: flake-heaped how or whence,
The structure of that succourable cloud,
What matter? Shamed she plunged into its shroud.   40

Orbed—so the woman-figure poets call
Because of rounds on rounds—that apple-shaped
Head which its hair binds close into a ball
Each side the curving ears—that pure undraped
Pout of the sister paps—that ... Once for all,
Say—her consummate circle thus escaped
With its innumerous circlets, sank absorbed,
Safe in the cloud—O naked Moon full-orbed!

But what means this? The downy swathes combine,
Conglobe, the smothery coy-caressing stuff   50
Curdles about her! Vain each twist and twine
Those lithe limbs try, encroached on by a fluff
Fitting as close as fits the dented spine
Its flexile ivory outside-flesh: enough!
The plumy drifts contract, condense, constringe,
Till she is swallowed by the feathery springe.

As when a pearl slips lost in the thin foam
Churned on a sea-shore, and, o'er-frothed, conceits

Herself safe-housed in Amphitrite's dome, —
If, through the bladdery wave-worked yeast, she
    meets   60
What most she loathes and leaps from, —elf from
    gnome
No gladlier, —finds that safest of retreats
Bubble about a treacherous hand wide ope
To grasp her—(divers who pick pearls so grope)—

So lay this Maid-Moon clasped around and caught
By rough red Pan, the god of all that tract:
He it was schemed the snare thus subtly wrought
With simulated earth-breath, —wool-tufts packed
Into a billowy wrappage. Sheep far-sought
For spotless shearings yield such: take the fact   70
As learned Virgil gives it, —how the breed
Whitens itself for ever: yes, indeed!

If one forefather ram, though pure as chalk
From tinge on fleece, should still display a tongue
Black 'neath the beast's moist palate, prompt men
    baulk
The propagating plague: he gets no young:
They rather slay him, —sell his hide to caulk
Ships with, first steeped in pitch, —nor hands are
    wrung
In sorrow for his fate: protected thus,
The purity we love is gained for us.   80

So did Girl-moon, by just her attribute
Of unmatched modesty betrayed, lie trapped,
Bruised to the breast of Pan, half-god half-brute,
Raked by his bristly boar-sward while he lapped
—Never say, kissed her! that were to pollute
Love's language—which moreover proves unapt

To tell how she recoiled—as who finds thorns
Where she sought flowers—when, feeling, she
　　　　touched—horns!

Then—does the legend say?—first moon-eclipse
Happened, first swooning-fit which puzzled sore　　　90
The early sages? Is that why she dips
Into the dark, a minute and no more,
Only so long as serves her while she rips
The cloud's womb through and, faultless as before,
Pursues her way? No lesson for a maid
Left she, a maid herself thus trapped, betrayed?

Ha, Virgil? Tell the rest, you! "To the deep
Of his domain the wildwood, Pan forthwith
Called her, and so she followed"—in her sleep,
Surely?—"by no means spurning him." The myth　　　100
Explain who may! Let all else go, I keep
—As of a ruin just a monolith—
Thus much, one verse of five words, each a boon:
Arcadia, night, a cloud, Pan, and the moon.

LOVE POEMS

BROWNING IS ONE of England's great love poets. Although he seldom speaks in his own voice, his love poetry possesses a wide range, from supreme happiness to jealous hatred. The emotional subtlety of his language captures the complex moods of love, while he is always alive to the tensions within a sexual relationship.

A few of his poems celebrate the vibrant joy of being in love, the excitement of meeting a lover, and the pleasure of sexual fulfilment. These are simply expressed, often with a lyric freshness. Most are seen from a male point of view, with the woman little more than a secondary figure. A poem like "Now," almost frantic in its desire to perpetuate a sensual pleasure, uses the passive woman quite deliberately. Browning in this poem expresses the difficulty the speaker finds in obtaining a relationship beyond the sensual, the problem he experiences in trying to make the moment eternal. The woman is completely buried under male rhetoric.

Browning's best love poems are those of search and failure. The search is for the good minute, that moment of mutual understanding which will ratify a deeper relationship, in which both lovers give themselves openly to each other. The search too often ends in failure. Browning's love poetry is full of doubts and self-questioning, as his speakers probe the causes of their failure. "Love among the Ruins" and "Two in the Campagna" illustrate this well. Both poems are set in the countryside amid the ruins of an earlier civilization, and in both, the landscape, consciously or unconsciously, is related to the speaker's feelings. A similar situation exists in "In the Doorway," where the barren scenery reflects the woman's cold relationship with her husband.

The language of the game of love appeals to Browning. Like Chaucer he appreciates the psychology men and women employ in their attempt to assert themselves and dominate their partners. This need for mastery can best be seen in "A Woman's Last Word" where, in the act of capitulating, the speaker subtly reinforces her power over her lover. The verbal tricks she uses can be seen in a less subtle form in "The Lost Mistress" where the rejected man refuses to give in, and, in bidding farewell, leaves room for possible reconciliation.

Many of Browning's love poems are set within a dramatic framework. Each of the last poems in this section has a strong plot and is concerned with a decisive moment in the speaker's life. A dying man rejecting a priest in the sickroom, an elderly man sightseeing with a younger woman, a young man waiting all night outside the villa of an obdurate girl: each situation is vividly drawn and each speaker's feelings are in tune with the surroundings in which he finds himself. The three poems were written during a period of thirty-five years, but together they demonstrate some of the recurring features of Browning's love poetry. They deal with unusual but convincing aspects of love, with strong sexual feelings, and with the frustrations and the limitations of human physicality.

SONG.

I.

Nay but you, who do not love her,
　Is she not pure gold, my mistress?
Holds earth aught—speak truth—above her?
　Aught like this tress, see, and this tress,
And this last fairest tress of all,
So fair, see, ere I let it fall?

II.

Because, you spend your lives in praising;
　To praise, you search the wide world over:
Then why not witness, calmly gazing,
　If earth holds aught—speak truth—above her?　10
Above this tress, and this, I touch
But cannot praise, I love so much!

ASK NOT ONE LEAST WORD OF PRAISE.

Ask not one least word of praise!
　Words declare your eyes are bright?
What then meant that summer day's
Silence spent in one long gaze?
　Was my silence wrong or right?

Words of praise were all to seek!
　Face of you and form of you,

Did they find the praise so weak
When my lips just touched your cheek—
   Touch which let my soul come through?   10

MEETING AT NIGHT.

I.

THE grey sea and the long black land;
And the yellow half-moon large and low;
And the startled little waves that leap
In fiery ringlets from their sleep,
As I gain the cove with pushing prow,
And quench its speed i' the slushy sand.

II.

Then a mile of warm sea-scented beach;
Three fields to cross till a farm appears;
A tap at the pane, the quick sharp scratch
And blue spurt of a lighted match,   10
And a voice less loud, thro' its joys and fears,
Than the two hearts beating each to each!

PARTING AT MORNING.

ROUND the cape of a sudden came the sea,
And the sun looked over the mountain's rim:
And straight was a path of gold for him,
And the need of a world of men for me.

NOW

OUT of your whole life give but a moment!
All of your life that has gone before,
All to come after it, — so you ignore
So you make perfect the present, — condense,
In a rapture of rage, for perfection's endowment,
Thought and feeling and soul and sense —
Merged in a moment which gives me at last
You around me for once, you beneath me, above
          me —
Me — sure that despite of time future, time past, —
This tick of our life-time's one moment you love me!   10
How long such suspension may linger? Ah, Sweet —
The moment eternal — just that and no more —
When ecstasy's utmost we clutch at the core
While cheeks burn, arms open, eyes shut and lips
          meet!

LOVE AMONG THE RUINS.

I.

WHERE the quiet-coloured end of evening smiles,
          Miles and miles
On the solitary pastures where our sheep
          Half-asleep
Tinkle homeward thro' the twilight, stray or stop
          As they crop —
Was the site once of a city great and gay,
          (So they say)

Of our country's very capital, its prince
          Ages since   10
Held his court in, gathered councils, wielding far
          Peace or war.

II.

Now, — the country does not even boast a tree,
          As you see,
To distinguish slopes of verdure, certain rills
          From the hills
Intersect and give a name to, (else they run
          Into one)
Where the domed and daring palace shot its spires
          Up like fires   20
O'er the hundred-gated circuit of a wall
          Bounding all,
Made of marble, men might march on nor be pressed,
          Twelve abreast.

III.

And such plenty and perfection, see, of grass
          Never was!
Such a carpet as, this summer-time, o'erspreads
          And embeds
Every vestige of the city, guessed alone,
          Stock or stone—   30
Where a multitude of men breathed joy and woe
          Long ago;
Lust of glory pricked their hearts up, dread of shame
          Struck them tame;
And that glory and that shame alike, the gold
          Bought and sold.

IV.

Now, —the single little turret that remains
       On the plains,
By the caper overrooted, by the gourd
       Overscored,   40
While the patching houseleek's head of blossom winks
       Through the chinks—
Marks the basement whence a tower in ancient time
       Sprang sublime,
And a burning ring, all round, the chariots traced
       As they raced,
And the monarch and his minions and his dames
       Viewed the games.

V.

And I know, while thus the quiet-coloured eve
       Smiles to leave   50
To their folding, all our many-tinkling fleece
       In such peace,
And the slopes and rills in undistinguished grey
       Melt away—
That a girl with eager eyes and yellow hair
       Waits me there
In the turret whence the charioteers caught soul
       For the goal,
When the king looked, where she looks now, breath-
       less, dumb
       Till I come.   60

VI.

But he looked upon the city, every side,
       Far and wide,
All the mountains topped with temples, all the glades'
       Colonnades,

All the causeys, bridges, aqueducts,—and then,
    All the men!
When I do come, she will speak not, she will stand,
    Either hand
On my shoulder, give her eyes the first embrace
    Of my face,   70
Ere we rush, ere we extinguish sight and speech
    Each on each.

VII.

In one year they sent a million fighters forth
    South and North,
And they built their gods a brazen pillar high
    As the sky,
Yet reserved a thousand chariots in full force—
    Gold, of course.
Oh heart! oh blood that freezes, blood that burns!
    Earth's returns   80
For whole centuries of folly, noise and sin!
    Shut them in,
With their triumphs and their glories and the rest!
    Love is best.

TWO IN THE CAMPAGNA.

I.

I WONDER do you feel to-day
  As I have felt since, hand in hand,
We sat down on the grass, to stray
  In spirit better through the land,
This morn of Rome and May?

II.

For me, I touched a thought, I know,
   Has tantalized me many times,
(Like turns of thread the spiders throw
   Mocking across our path) for rhymes
To catch at and let go.   10

III.

Help me to hold it! First it left
   The yellowing fennel, run to seed
There, branching from the brickwork's cleft,
   Some old tomb's ruin: yonder weed
Took up the floating weft,

IV.

Where one small orange cup amassed
   Five beetles, — blind and green they grope
Among the honey-meal: and last,
   Everywhere on the grassy slope
I traced it. Hold it fast!   20

V.

The champaign with its endless fleece
   Of feathery grasses everywhere!
Silence and passion, joy and peace,
   An everlasting wash of air —
Rome's ghost since her decease.

VI.

Such life here, through such lengths of hours,
   Such miracles performed in play,

Two in the Campagna

The Campagna

Such primal naked forms of flowers,
    Such letting nature have her way
While heaven looks from its towers!   30

                    VII.

How say you? Let us, O my dove,
    Let us be unashamed of soul,
As earth lies bare to heaven above!
    How is it under our control
To love or not to love?

                    VIII.

I would that you were all to me,
    You that are just so much, no more.
Nor yours nor mine, nor slave nor free!
    Where does the fault lie? What the core
O' the wound, since wound must be?   40

                    IX.

I would I could adopt your will,
    See with your eyes, and set my heart
Beating by yours, and drink my fill
    At your soul's springs, — your part my part
In life, for good and ill.

                    X.

No. I yearn upward, touch you close,
    Then stand away. I kiss your cheek,
Catch your soul's warmth, —I pluck the rose
    And love it more than tongue can speak—
Then the good minute goes.   50

XI.

Already how am I so far
　　Out of that minute? Must I go
Still like the thistle-ball, no bar,
　　Onward, whenever light winds blow,
Fixed by no friendly star?

XII.

Just when I seemed about to learn!
　　Where is the thread now? Off again!
The old trick! Only I discern—
　　Infinite passion, and the pain
Of finite hearts that yearn.　　　　　　　60

IN THE DOORWAY.

I.

THE swallow has set her six young on the rail,
　　　　And looks sea-ward:
The water's in stripes like a snake, olive-pale
　　　　To the leeward, —
On the weather-side, black, spotted white with the wind.
"Good fortune departs, and disaster's behind,"—
Hark, the wind with its wants and its infinite wail!

II.

Our fig-tree, that leaned for the saltness, has furled
　　　　Her five fingers,
Each leaf like a hand opened wide to the world　　10
　　　　Where there lingers

No glint of the gold, Summer sent for her sake:
How the vines writhe in rows, each impaled on its stake!
My heart shrivels up and my spirit shrinks curled.

III.

Yet here are we two; we have love, house enough,
          With the field there,
This house of four rooms, that field red and rough,
          Though it yield there,
For the rabbit that robs, scarce a blade or a bent;
If a magpie alight now, it seems an event;   20
And they both will be gone at November's rebuff.

IV.

But why must cold spread? but wherefore bring change
          To the spirit,
God meant should mate his with an infinite range,
          And inherit
His power to put life in the darkness and cold?
Oh, live and love worthily, bear and be bold!
Whom Summer made friends of, let Winter estrange!

A WOMAN'S LAST WORD.

I.

LET'S contend no more, Love,
          Strive nor weep:
All be as before, Love,
     · —Only sleep!

II.

What so wild as words are?
    I and thou
In debate, as birds are,
    Hawk on bough!

III.

See the creature stalking
    While we speak!   10
Hush and hide the talking,
    Cheek on cheek!

IV.

What so false as truth is,
    False to thee?
Where the serpent's tooth is
    Shun the tree—

V.

Where the apple reddens
    Never pry—
Lest we lose our Edens,
    Eve and I.   20

VI.

Be a god and hold me
    With a charm!
Be a man and fold me
    With thine arm!

VII.

Teach me, only teach, Love!
  As I ought
I will speak thy speech, Love,
  Think thy thought—

VIII.

Meet, if thou require it,
  Both demands,
Laying flesh and spirit
  In thy hands.

30

IX.

That shall be to-morrow
  Not to-night:
I must bury sorrow
  Out of sight:

X.

—Must a little weep, Love,
  (Foolish me!)
And so fall asleep, Love,
  Loved by thee.

40

THE LOST MISTRESS.

I.

ALL's over, then: does truth sound bitter
  As one at first believes?

Hark, 'tis the swallows' good-night twitter
   About your cottage eaves!

II.

And the leaf-buds on the vine are woolly,
   I noticed that, today;
One day more bursts them open fully
   — You know the red turns grey.

III.

Tomorrow we meet the same then, dearest?
   May I take your hand in mine?   10
Mere friends are we, — well, friends the merest
   Keep much that I resign:

IV.

For each glance of the eye so bright and black,
   Though I keep with heart's endeavour, —
Your voice, when you wish the snowdrops back,
   Though it stay in my soul for ever! —

V.

Yet I will but say what mere friends say,
   Or only a thought stronger;
I will hold your hand but as long as all may,
   Or so very little longer!   20

The Lost Mistress

Robert Browning Aged 76

CONFESSIONS.

I.

WHAT is he buzzing in my ears?
  "Now that I come to die,
"Do I view the world as a vale of tears?"
  Ah, reverend sir, not I!

II.

What I viewed there once, what I view again
  Where the physic bottles stand
On the table's edge, —is a suburb lane,
  With a wall to my bedside hand.

III.

That lane sloped, much as the bottles do,
  From a house you could descry
O'er the garden-wall: is the curtain blue
  Or green to a healthy eye?

IV.

To mine, it serves for the old June weather
  Blue above lane and wall;
And that farthest bottle labelled "Ether"
  Is the house o'ertopping all.

V.

At a terrace, somewhere near the stopper,
   There watched for me, one June,
A girl: I know, sir, it's improper,
   My poor mind's out of tune.   20

VI.

Only, there was a way ... you crept
   Close by the side, to dodge
Eyes in the house, two eyes except:
   They styled their house "The Lodge."

VII.

What right had a lounger up their lane?
   But, by creeping very close,
With the good wall's help,—their eyes might strain
   And stretch themselves to Oes,

VIII.

Yet never catch her and me together,
   As she left the attic, there,   30.
By the rim of the bottle labelled "Ether,"
   And stole from stair to stair,

IX.

And stood by the rose-wreathed gate. Alas,
   We loved, sir—used to meet:
How sad and bad and mad it was—
   But then, how it was sweet!

INAPPREHENSIVENESS.

WE two stood simply friend-like side by side,
Viewing a twilight country far and wide,
Till she at length broke silence. "How it towers
Yonder, the ruin o'er this vale of ours!
The West's faint flare behind it so relieves
Its rugged outline—sight perhaps deceives,
Or I could almost fancy that I see
A branch wave plain—belike some wind-sown tree
Chance-rooted where a missing turret was.
What would I give for the perspective glass   10
At home, to make out if 't is really so!
Has Ruskin noticed here at Asolo
That certain weed-growths on the ravaged wall
Seem" ... something that I could not say at all,
My thought being rather—as absorbed she sent
Look onward after look from eyes distent
With longing to reach Heaven's gate left ajar—
"Oh, fancies that might be, oh, facts that are!
What of a wilding? By you stands, and may
So stand unnoticed till the Judgment Day,   20
One who, if once aware that your regard
Claimed what his heart holds,—woke, as from its sward
The flower, the dormant passion, so to speak—
Then what a rush of life would startling wreak
Revenge on your inapprehensive stare
While, from the ruin and the West's faint flare,
You let your eyes meet mine, touch what you term
Quietude—that's an universe in germ—
The dormant passion needing but a look
To burst into immense life!"
                              "No, the book   30

Which noticed how the wall-growths wave" said she
"Was not by Ruskin."
                          I said "Vernon Lee?"

A SERENADE AT THE VILLA.

I.

THAT was I, you heard last night,
    When there rose no moon at all,
Nor, to pierce the strained and tight
    Tent of heaven, a planet small:
Life was dead and so was light.

II.

Not a twinkle from the fly,
    Not a glimmer from the worm;
When the crickets stopped their cry,
    When the owls forbore a term,
You heard music; that was I.   10

III.

Earth turned in her sleep with pain,
    Sultrily suspired for proof:
In at heaven and out again,
    Lightning!—where it broke the roof,
Bloodlike, some few drops of rain.

IV.

What they could my words expressed,
    O my love, my all, my one!

Singing helped the verses best,
    And when singing's best was done,
To my lute I left the rest.   20

V.

So wore night; the East was grey,
    White the broad-faced hemlock-flowers:
There would be another day;
    Ere its first of heavy hours
Found me, I had passed away.

VI.

What became of all the hopes,
    Words and song and lute as well?
Say, this struck you—"When life gropes
    "Feebly for the path where fell
"Light last on the evening slopes,   30

VII.

"One friend in that path shall be,
    "To secure my step from wrong;
"One to count night day for me,
    "Patient through the watches long,
"Serving most with none to see."

VIII.

Never say—as something bodes—
    "So, the worst has yet a worse!
"When life halts 'neath double loads,
    "Better the taskmaster's curse
"Than such music on the roads!   40

IX.

"When no moon succeeds the sun,
   "Nor can pierce the midnight's tent
"Any star, the smallest one,
   "While some drops, where lightning rent,
"Show the final storm begun—

X.

"When the fire-fly hides its spot,
   "When the garden-voices fail
"In the darkness thick and hot, —
   "Shall another voice avail,
"That shape be where these are not?   50

XI.

"Has some plague a longer lease,
   "Proffering its help uncouth?
"Can't one even die in peace?
   "As one shuts one's eyes on youth,
"Is that face the last one sees?"

XII.

Oh how dark your villa was,
   Windows fast and obdurate!
How the garden grudged me grass
   Where I stood—the iron gate
Ground its teeth to let me pass!   60

DRAMATIC MONOLOGUES

THE DRAMATIC MONOLOGUE is Browning's chief contribution to English poetry. He had a strong historical sense and a dramatist's command of speech rhythms, yet his stage plays were failures because he found it difficult to write convincing dialogue. His characters too often speak at, rather than with, each other. One frequently feels they would be happier in a court-room than in a theatre. The dramatic monologue is, therefore, a form which capitalizes on Browning's strengths and minimizes his weaknesses. It gives his men and women the freedom to talk without fear of interruption and allows each speaker to become his own lawyer.

Although there are certain common features, no dramatic monologue is exactly the same. Each is a single speech, usually directed towards a silent listener whose presence and response is clearly suggested. (In a few poems the speaker talks *about* the second person rather than to him.) The speech happens at a dramatic moment, usually towards the end of the action, so there is much recapitulation. The setting is often vividly created during the course of the monologue.

The reader becomes an eavesdropper on the edge of the action—an unseen observer, fascinated by the unusual character he overhears. But his role is not passive. He must be alert, ready to evaluate what is being said, because Browning's speakers are nearly all casuists or apologists, and are seldom what they seem. Their public pronouncements are warped by their inner pressures and needs. Their words, intended to

75

convince their listener, frequently betray their limitations, their insecurity, their frustrations or fears. They always talk too much: the longer they speak, the more they reveal about themselves.

Browning's monologues range over a thousand years, from Rome at the time of Christ to Victorian England, via eighteenth-century Venice. But the best remembered and the most imaginatively conceived are those set in Renaissance Italy. The paradoxes and extremes of the Renaissance world present Browning with rich material. In particular, he exploited the moral ambiguity, that blend of the sacred and venal, high artistic ideals and corrupt living, which characterize so many of its artists and churchmen. Yet Browning is no Victorian moralist pointing his finger at sins and follies. Many of his characters are attractive as human beings, whatever their failings. Browning often creates a tension between his reader's sympathy and his judgment. At times we are almost taken in by a charlatan; at others we forgive a rogue.

The dramatic monologue, with its relativist stances and special pleadings, was the ideal medium for Browning's poetic gifts. "I only make men and women speak," he wrote to Elizabeth Barrett, "give you truth broken into prismatic hues, and fear the pure white light, even if it is in me." The truth is there in the dramatic monologues, but the reader has to discover it for himself.

MY LAST DUCHESS.

FERRARA

THAT's my last Duchess painted on the wall,
Looking as if she were alive. I call
That piece a wonder, now: Frà Pandolf's hands
Worked busily a day, and there she stands.
Will 't please you sit and look at her? I said
"Frà Pandolf" by design, for never read
Strangers like you that pictured countenance,
The depth and passion of its earnest glance,
But to myself they turned (since none puts by
The curtain I have drawn for you, but I)   10
And seemed as they would ask me, if they durst,
How such a glance came there; so, not the first
Are you to turn and ask thus. Sir, 't was not
Her husband's presence only, called that spot
Of joy into the Duchess' cheek: perhaps
Frà Pandolf chanced to say "Her mantle laps
"Over my lady's wrist too much," or "Paint
"Must never hope to reproduce the faint
"Half-flush that dies along her throat:" such stuff
Was courtesy, she thought, and cause enough   20
For calling up that spot of joy. She had
A heart—how shall I say?—too soon made glad,
Too easily impressed; she liked whate'er
She looked on, and her looks went everywhere.
Sir, 't was all one! My favour at her breast,
The dropping of the daylight in the West,
The bough of cherries some officious fool
Broke in the orchard for her, the white mule
She rode with round the terrace—all and each
Would draw from her alike the approving speech,   30

Or blush, at least. She thanked men,—good! but
    thanked
Somehow—I know not how—as if she ranked
My gift of a nine-hundred-years-old name
With anybody's gift. Who'd stoop to blame
This sort of trifling? Even had you skill
In speech—(which I have not)—to make your will
Quite clear to such an one, and say, "Just this
"Or that in you disgusts me; here you miss,
"Or there exceed the mark"—and if she let
Herself be lessoned so, nor plainly set   40
Her wits to yours, forsooth, and made excuse,
—E'en then would be some stooping; and I choose
Never to stoop. Oh sir, she smiled, no doubt,
Whene'er I passed her; but who passed without
Much the same smile? This grew; I gave commands;
Then all smiles stopped together. There she stands
As if alive. Will 't please you rise? We'll meet
The company below, then. I repeat,
The Count your master's known munificence
Is ample warrant that no just pretence   50
Of mine for dowry will be disallowed;
Though his fair daughter's self, as I avowed
At starting, is my object. Nay, we'll go
Together down, sir. Notice Neptune, though,
Taming a sea-horse, thought a rarity,
Which Claus of Innsbruck cast in bronze for me!

PORPHYRIA'S LOVER.

THE rain set early in to-night,
    The sullen wind was soon awake,
It tore the elm-tops down for spite,
    And did its worst to vex the lake:

My Last Duchess

Soliloquy of the Spanish Cloister

I listened with heart fit to break.
When glided in Porphyria; straight
  She shut the cold out and the storm,
And kneeled and made the cheerless grate
  Blaze up, and all the cottage warm;
  Which done, she rose, and from her form   10
Withdrew the dripping cloak and shawl,
  And laid her soiled gloves by, untied
Her hat and let the damp hair fall,
  And, last, she sat down by my side
  And called me. When no voice replied,
She put my arm about her waist,
  And made her smooth white shoulder bare,
And all her yellow hair displaced,
  And, stooping, made my cheek lie there,
  And spread, o'er all, her yellow hair,   20
Murmuring how she loved me—she
  Too weak, for all her heart's endeavour,
To set its struggling passion free
  From pride, and vainer ties dissever,
  And give herself to me for ever.
But passion sometimes would prevail,
  Nor could to-night's gay feast restrain
A sudden thought of one so pale
  For love of her, and all in vain:
  So, she was come through wind and rain.   30
Be sure I looked up at her eyes
  Happy and proud; at last I knew
Porphyria worshipped me; surprise
  Made my heart swell, and still it grew
  While I debated what to do.
That moment she was mine, mine, fair,
  Perfectly pure and good: I found
A thing to do, and all her hair
  In one long yellow string I wound
  Three times her little throat around,   40

And strangled her. No pain felt she;
   I am quite sure she felt no pain.
As a shut bud that holds a bee,
   I warily oped her lids: again
   Laughed the blue eyes without a stain.
And I untightened next the tress
   About her neck; her cheek once more
Blushed bright beneath my burning kiss:
   I propped her head up as before,
   Only, this time my shoulder bore   50
Her head, which droops upon it still:
   The smiling rosy little head,
So glad it has its utmost will,
   That all it scorned at once is fled,
   And I, its love, am gained instead!
Porphyria's love: she guessed not how
   Her darling one wish would be heard.
And thus we sit together now,
   And all night long we have not stirred,
   And yet God has not said a word!   60

SOLILOQUY OF THE SPANISH CLOISTER.

I.

GR-R-R—there go, my heart's abhorrence!
   Water your damned flower-pots, do!
If hate killed men, Brother Lawrence,
   God's blood, would not mine kill you!
What? your myrtle-bush wants trimming?
   Oh, that rose has prior claims—
Needs its leaden vase filled brimming?
   Hell dry you up with its flames!

II.

At the meal we sit together:
   Salve tibi!   I must hear   10
Wise talk of the kind of weather,
   Sort of season, time of year:
Not a plenteous cork-crop: scarcely
   Dare we hope oak-galls, I doubt:
What's the Latin name for "parsley"?
   What's the Greek name for Swine's Snout?

III.

Whew! We'll have our platter burnished,
   Laid with care on our own shelf!
With a fire-new spoon we're furnished,
   And a goblet for ourself,   20
Rinsed like something sacrificial
   Ere 't is fit to touch our chaps—
Marked with L. for our initial!
   (He-he! There his lily snaps!)

IV.

Saint, forsooth! While brown Dolores
   Squats outside the Convent bank
With Sanchicha, telling stories,
   Steeping tresses in the tank,
Blue-black, lustrous, thick like horsehairs,
   —Can't I see his dead eye glow,   30
Bright as 't were a Barbary corsair's?
   (That is, if he'd let it show!)

V.

When he finishes refection,
   Knife and fork he never lays

Cross-wise, to my recollection,
    As do I, in Jesu's praise.
I the Trinity illustrate,
    Drinking watered orange-pulp—
In three sips the Arian frustrate;
    While he drains his at one gulp.   40

VI.

Oh, those melons? If he's able
    We're to have a feast! so nice!
One goes to the Abbot's table,
    All of us get each a slice.
How go on your flowers? None double?
    Not one fruit-sort can you spy?
Strange!—And I, too, at such trouble,
    Keep them close-nipped on the sly!

VII.

There's a great text in Galatians,
    Once you trip on it, entails   50
Twenty-nine distinct damnations,
    One sure, if another fails:
If I trip him just a-dying,
    Sure of heaven as sure can be,
Spin him round and send him flying
    Off to hell, a Manichee?

VIII.

Or, my scrofulous French novel
    On grey paper with blunt type!
Simply glance at it, you grovel
    Hand and foot in Belial's gripe: 60
If I double down its pages

At the woeful sixteenth print,
When he gathers his greengages,
  Ope a sieve and slip it in 't?

IX.

Or, there's Satan!—one might venture
  Pledge one's soul to him, yet leave
Such a flaw in the indenture
  As he'd miss till, past retrieve,
Blasted lay that rose-acacia
  We're so proud of!   *Hy, Zy, Hine* ...   70
'St, there's Vespers!   *Plena gratiâ*
  Ave, Virgo!   Gr-r-r—you swine!

A TOCCATA OF GALUPPI'S.

I.

OH Galuppi, Baldassaro, this is very sad to find!
I can hardly misconceive you; it would prove me deaf
    and blind;
But although I take your meaning, 't is with such a heavy
    mind!

II.

Here you come with your old music, and here's all the
    good it brings.
What, they lived once thus at Venice where the merchants
    were the kings,
Where Saint Mark's is, where the Doges used to wed the
    sea with rings?

III.

Ay, because the sea's the street there; and 't is arched
        by . . . what you call
. . . Shylock's bridge with houses on it, where they kept
        the carnival:
I was never out of England—it's as if I saw it all.

IV.

Did young people take their pleasure when the sea was
        warm in May?   10
Balls and masks begun at midnight, burning ever to mid-
        day,
When they made up fresh adventures for the morrow,
        do you say?

V.

Was a lady such a lady, cheeks so round and lips so
        red,—
On her neck the small face buoyant, like a bell-flower on
        its bed,
O'er the breast's superb abundance where a man might
        base his head?

VI.

Well, and it was graceful of them—they'd break talk off
        and afford
—She, to bite her mask's black velvet—he, to finger on
        his sword,
While you sat and played Toccatas, stately at the clavi-
        chord?

VII.

What? Those lesser thirds so plaintive, sixths diminished,
    sigh on sigh,
Told them something? Those suspensions, those solu-
    tions—"Must we die?"   20
Those commiserating sevenths—"Life might last! we
    can but try!"

VIII.

"Were you happy?"—"Yes."—"And are you still as
    happy?"—"Yes. And you?"
—"Then, more kisses!"—"Did *I* stop them, when a
    million seemed so few?"
Hark, the dominant's persistence till it must be an-
    swered to!

IX.

So, an octave struck the answer. Oh, they praised you,
    I dare say!
"Brave Galuppi! that was music! good alike at grave
    and gay!
"I can always leave off talking when I hear a master
    play!"

X.

Then they left you for their pleasure: till in due time,
    one by one,
Some with lives that came to nothing, some with deeds
    as well undone,
Death stepped tacitly and took them where they never
    see the sun.   30

XI.

But when I sit down to reason, think to take my stand
      nor swerve,
While I triumph o'er a secret wrung from nature's close
      reserve,
In you come with your cold music till I creep thro' every
      nerve.

XII.

. Yes, you, like a ghostly cricket, creaking where a house
      was burned:
"Dust and ashes, dead and done with, Venice spent what
      Venice earned.
"The soul, doubtless, is immortal—where a soul can be
      discerned.

XIII.

"Yours for instance: you know physics, something of
      geology,
"Mathematics are your pastime; souls shall rise in their
      degree;
"Butterflies may dread extinction,—you'll not die, it
      cannot be!

XIV.

"As for Venice and her people, merely born to bloom
      and drop,   40
"Here on earth they bore their fruitage, mirth and folly
      were the crop:
"What of soul was left, I wonder, when the kissing had
      to stop?

XV.

"Dust and ashes!" So you creak it, and I want the
    heart to scold.
Dear dead women, with such hair, too—what's become
    of all the gold
Used to hang and brush their bosoms? I feel chilly and
    grown old.

THE BISHOP ORDERS HIS TOMB AT
SAINT PRAXED'S CHURCH.

ROME, 15—.

VANITY, saith the preacher, vanity!
Draw round my bed: is Anselm keeping back?
Nephews—sons mine . . . ah God, I know not! Well—
She, men would have to be your mother once,
Old Gandolf envied me, so fair she was!
What's done is done, and she is dead beside,
Dead long ago, and I am Bishop since,
And as she died so must we die ourselves,
And thence ye may perceive the world's a dream.
Life, how and what is it? As here I lie   10
In this state-chamber, dying by degrees,
Hours and long hours in the dead night, I ask
"Do I live, am I dead?" Peace, peace seems all.
Saint Praxed's ever was the church for peace;
And so, about this tomb of mine. I fought
With tooth and nail to save my niche, ye know:
—Old Gandolf cozened me, despite my care;
Shrewd was that snatch from out the corner South
He graced his carrion with, God curse the same!
Yet still my niche is not so cramped but thence   20
One sees the pulpit o' the epistle-side,

And somewhat of the choir, those silent seats,
And up into the aery dome where live
The angels, and a sunbeam's sure to lurk:
And I shall fill my slab of basalt there,
And 'neath my tabernacle take my rest,
With those nine columns round me, two and two,
The odd one at my feet where Anselm stands:
Peach-blossom marble all, the rare, the ripe
As fresh-poured red wine of a mighty pulse.   30
—Old Gandolf with his paltry onion-stone,
Put me where I may look at him! True peach,
Rosy and flawless: how I earned the prize!
Draw close: that conflagration of my church
—What then? So much was saved if aught were missed!
My sons, ye would not be my death? Go dig
The white-grape vineyard where the oil-press stood,
Drop water gently till the surface sink,
And if ye find ... Ah God, I know not, I! ...
Bedded in store of rotten fig-leaves soft,   40
And corded up in a tight olive-frail,
Some lump, ah God, of *lapis lazuli*,
Big as a Jew's head cut off at the nape,
Blue as a vein o'er the Madonna's breast ...
Sons, all have I bequeathed you, villas, all,
That brave Frascati villa with its bath,
So, let the blue lump poise between my knees,
Like God the Father's globe on both his hands
Ye worship in the Jesu Church so gay,
For Gandolf shall not choose but see and burst!   50
Swift as a weaver's shuttle fleet our years:
Man goeth to the grave, and where is he?
Did I say basalt for my slab, sons? Black—
'T was ever antique-black I meant! How else
Shall ye contrast my frieze to come beneath?
The bas-relief in bronze ye promised me,
Those Pans and Nymphs ye wot of, and perchance

Some tripod, thyrsus, with a vase or so,
The Saviour at his sermon on the mount,
Saint Praxed in a glory, and one Pan   60
Ready to twitch the Nymph's last garment off,
And Moses with the tables ... but I know
Ye mark me not! What do they whisper thee,
Child of my bowels, Anselm? Ah, ye hope
To revel down my villas while I gasp
Bricked o'er with beggar's mouldy travertine
Which Gandolf from his tomb-top chuckles at!
Nay, boys, ye love me—all of jasper, then!
'T is jasper ye stand pledged to, lest I grieve
My bath must needs be left behind, alas!   70
One block, pure green as a pistachio-nut,
There's plenty jasper somewhere in the world—
And have I not Saint Praxed's ear to pray
Horses for ye, and brown Greek manuscripts,
And mistresses with great smooth marbly limbs?
—That's if ye carve my epitaph aright,
Choice Latin, picked phrase, Tully's every word,
No gaudy ware like Gandolf's second line—
Tully, my masters? Ulpian serves his need!
And then how I shall lie through centuries,   80
And hear the blessed mutter of the mass,
And see God made and eaten all day long,
And feel the steady candle-flame, and taste
Good strong thick stupefying incense-smoke!
For as I lie here, hours of the dead night,
Dying in state and by such slow degrees,
I fold my arms as if they clasped a crook,
And stretch my feet forth straight as stone can point,
And let the bedclothes, for a mortcloth, drop
Into great laps and folds of sculptor's-work: 90
And as yon tapers dwindle, and strange thoughts
Grow, with a certain humming in my ears,
About the life before I lived this life,

And this life too, popes, cardinals and priests,
Saint Praxed at his sermon on the mount,
Your tall pale mother with her talking eyes,
And new-found agate urns as fresh as day,
And marble's language, Latin pure, discreet,
—Aha, ELUCESCEBAT quoth our friend?
No Tully, said I, Ulpian at the best!   100
Evil and brief hath been my pilgrimage.
All *lapis*, all, sons! Else I give the Pope
My villas! Will ye ever eat my heart?
Ever your eyes were as a lizard's quick,
They glitter like your mother's for my soul,
Or ye would heighten my impoverished frieze,
Piece out its starved design, and fill my vase
With grapes, and add a vizor and a Term,
And to the tripod ye would tie a lynx
That in his struggle throws the thyrsus down,   110
To comfort me on my entablature
Whereon I am to lie till I must ask
"Do I live, am I dead?" There, leave me, there!
For ye have stabbed me with ingratitude
To death—ye wish it—God, ye wish it! Stone—
Gritstone, a-crumble! Clammy squares which sweat
As if the corpse they keep were oozing through—
And no more *lapis* to delight the world!
Well go! I bless ye. Fewer tapers there,
But in a row: and, going, turn your backs   120
–Ay, like departing altar-ministrants,
And leave me in my church, the church for peace,
That I may watch at leisure if he leers—
Old Gandolf, at me, from his onion-stone,
As still he envied me, so fair she was!

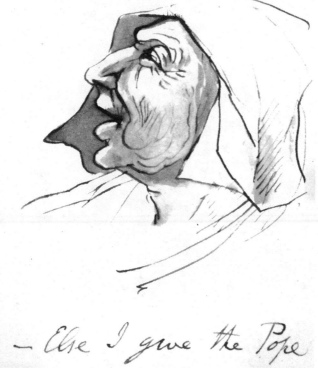

— Else I give the Pope
My Villas — —

The Dying Bishop

The Coronation of the Virgin

FRA LIPPO LIPPI.

I AM poor brother Lippo, by your leave!
You need not clap your torches to my face.
Zooks, what's to blame? you think you see a monk!
What, 't is past midnight, and you go the rounds,
And here you catch me at an alley's end
Where sportive ladies leave their doors ajar?
The Carmine's my cloister: hunt it up,
Do, —harry out, if you must show your zeal,
Whatever rat, there, haps on his wrong hole,
And nip each softling of a wee white mouse,   10
Weke, weke, that's crept to keep him company!
Aha, you know your betters! Then, you'll take
Your hand away that's fiddling on my throat,
And please to know me likewise. Who am I?
Why, one, sir, who is lodging with a friend
Three streets off—he's a certain ... how d' ye call?
Master—a ... Cosimo of the Medici,
I' the house that caps the corner. Boh! you were best!
Remember and tell me, the day you're hanged,
How you affected such a gullet's-gripe!   20
But you, sir, it concerns you that your knaves
Pick up a manner nor discredit you:
Zooks, are we pilchards, that they sweep the streets
And count fair prize what comes into their net?
He's Judas to a tittle, that man is!
Just such a face! Why, sir, you make amends.
Lord, I'm not angry! Bid your hangdogs go
Drink out this quarter-florin to the health
Of the munificent House that harbours me
(And many more beside, lads! more beside!)   30

And all's come square again. I'd like his face—
His, elbowing on his comrade in the door
With the pike and lantern,—for the slave that holds
John Baptist's head a-dangle by the hair
With one hand ("Look you, now," as who should say)
And his weapon in the other, yet unwiped!
It's not your chance to have a bit of chalk,
A wood-coal or the like? or you should see!
Yes, I'm the painter, since you style me so.
What, brother Lippo's doings, up and down,   40
You know them and they take you? like enough!
I saw the proper twinkle in your eye—
'Tell you, I liked your looks at very first.
Let's sit and set things straight now, hip to haunch.
Here's spring come, and the nights one makes up bands
To roam the town and sing out carnival,
And I've been three weeks shut within my mew,
A-painting for the great man, saints and saints
And saints again. I could not paint all night—
Ouf! I leaned out of window for fresh air.   50
There came a hurry of feet and little feet,
A sweep of lute-strings, laughs, and whifts of song,—
Flower o' the broom,
Take away love, and our earth is a tomb!
Flower o' the quince,
I let Lisa go, and what good in life since?
Flower o' the thyme—and so on. Round they went.
Scarce had they turned the corner when a titter
Like the skipping of rabbits by moonlight,—three slim
          shapes,
And a face that looked up ... zooks, sir, flesh and
          blood,   60
That's all I'm made of! Into shreds it went,
Curtain and counterpane and coverlet,
All the bed-furniture—a dozen knots,
There was a ladder! Down I let myself,

Hands and feet, scrambling somehow, and so dropped,
And after them. I came up with the fun
Hard by Saint Laurence, hail fellow, well met, —
Flower o' the rose,
If I've been merry, what matter who knows?
And so as I was stealing back again   70
To get to bed and have a bit of sleep
Ere I rise up to-morrow and go work
On Jerome knocking at his poor old breast
With his great round stone to subdue the flesh,
You snap me of the sudden. Ah, I see!
Though your eye twinkles still, you shake your head—
Mine's shaved—a monk, you say—the sting's in that!
If Master Cosimo announced himself,
Mum's the word naturally; but a monk!
Come, what am I a beast for? tell us, now!   80
I was a baby when my mother died
And father died and left me in the street.
I starved there, God knows how, a year or two
On fig-skins, melon-parings, rinds and shucks,
Refuse and rubbish. One fine frosty day,
My stomach being empty as your hat,
The wind doubled me up and down I went.
Old Aunt Lapaccia trussed me with one hand,
(Its fellow was a stinger as I knew)
And so along the wall, over the bridge,   90
By the straight cut to the convent. Six words there,
While I stood munching my first bread that month:
"So, boy, you're minded," quoth the good fat father
Wiping his own mouth, 't was refection-time, —
"To quit this very miserable world?
"Will you renounce" ... "the mouthful of bread?"
          thought I;
By no means! Brief, they made a monk of me;
I did renounce the world, its pride and greed,
Palace, farm, villa, shop and banking-house,

Trash, such as these poor devils of Medici   100
Have given their hearts to—all at eight years old.
Well, sir, I found in time, you may be sure,
'T was not for nothing—the good bellyful,
The warm serge and the rope that goes all round,
And day-long blessed idleness beside!
"Let's see what the urchin's fit for"—that came next.
Not overmuch their way, I must confess.
Such a to-do! They tried me with their books:
Lord, they'd have taught me Latin in pure waste!
Flower o' the clove,   110
All the Latin I construe is, "amo" I love!
But, mind you, when a boy starves in the streets
Eight years together, as my fortune was,
Watching folk's faces to know who will fling
The bit of half-stripped grape-bunch he desires,
And who will curse or kick him for his pains, —
Which gentleman processional and fine,
Holding a candle to the Sacrament,
Will wink and let him lift a plate and catch
The droppings of the wax to sell again,   120
Or holla for the Eight and have him whipped, —
How say I?—nay, which dog bites, which lets drop
His bone from the heap of offal in the street, —
Why, soul and sense of him grow sharp alike,
He learns the look of things, and none the less
For admonition from the hunger-pinch.
I had a store of such remarks, be sure,
Which, after I found leisure, turned to use.
I drew men's faces on my copy-books,
Scrawled them within the antiphonary's marge,   130
Joined legs and arms to the long music-notes,
Found eyes and nose and chin for A's and B's,
And made a string of pictures of the world
Betwixt the ins and outs of verb and noun,

On the wall, the bench, the door. The monks looked
    black.
"Nay," quoth the Prior, "turn him out, d' ye say?
"In no wise. Lose a crow and catch a lark.
"What if at last we get our man of parts,
"We Carmelites, like those Camaldolese
"And Preaching Friars, to do our church up fine   140
"And put the front on it that ought to be!"
And hereupon he bade me daub away.
Thank you! my head being crammed, the walls a blank,
Never was such prompt disemburdening.
First, every sort of monk, the black and white,
I drew them, fat and lean: then, folk at church,
From good old gossips waiting to confess
Their cribs of barrel-droppings, candle-ends, —
To the breathless fellow at the altar-foot,
Fresh from his murder, safe and sitting there   150
With the little children round him in a row
Of admiration, half for his beard and half
For that white anger of his victim's son
Shaking a fist at him with one fierce arm,
Signing himself with the other because of Christ
(Whose sad face on the cross sees only this
After the passion of a thousand years)
Till some poor girl, her apron o'er her head,
(Which the intense eyes looked through) came at eve
On tiptoe, said a word, dropped in a loaf,   160
Her pair of earrings and a bunch of flowers
(The brute took growling), prayed, and so was gone.
I painted all, then cried "'T is ask and have;
"Choose, for more's ready!"—laid the ladder flat,
And showed my covered bit of cloister-wall.
The monks closed in a circle and praised loud
Till checked, taught what to see and not to see,
Being simple bodies, —"That's the very man!

"Look at the boy who stoops to pat the dog!
"That woman's like the Prior's niece who comes   170
"To care about his asthma: it's the life!"
But there my triumph's straw-fire flared and funked;
Their betters took their turn to see and say:
The Prior and the learned pulled a face
And stopped all that in no time. "How? what's here?
"Quite from the mark of painting, bless us all!
"Faces, arms, legs and bodies like the true
"As much as pea and pea! it's devil's-game!
"Your business is not to catch men with show,
"With homage to the perishable clay,   180
"But lift them over it, ignore it all,
"Make them forget there's such a thing as flesh.
"Your business is to paint the souls of men—
"Man's soul, and it's a fire, smoke … no, it's not …
"It's vapour done up like a new-born babe—
"(In that shape when you die it leaves your mouth)
"It's … well, what matters talking, it's the soul!
"Give us no more of body than shows soul!
"Here's Giotto, with his Saint a-praising God,
"That sets us praising,—why not stop with him?   190
"Why put all thoughts of praise out of our head
"With wonder at lines, colours, and what not?
"Paint the soul, never mind the legs and arms!
"Rub all out, try at it a second time.
"Oh, that white smallish female with the breasts,
"She's just my niece … Herodias, I would say,—
"Who went and danced and got men's heads cut off!
"Have it all out!" Now, is this sense, I ask?
A fine way to paint soul, by painting body
So ill, the eye can't stop there, must go further   200
And can't fare worse! Thus, yellow does for white
When what you put for yellow's simply black,
And any sort of meaning looks intense

When all beside itself means and looks nought.
Why can't a painter lift each foot in turn,
Left foot and right foot, go a double step,
Make his flesh liker and his soul more like,
Both in their order? Take the prettiest face,
The Prior's niece ... patron-saint—is it so pretty
You can't discover if it means hope, fear,   210
Sorrow or joy? won't beauty go with these?
Suppose I've made her eyes all right and blue,
Can't I take breath and try to add life's flash,
And then add soul and heighten them threefold?
Or say there's beauty with no soul at all—
(I never saw it—put the case the same—)
If you get simple beauty and nought else,
You get about the best thing God invents:
That's somewhat: and you'll find the soul you have
        missed,
Within yourself, when you return him thanks.   220
"Rub all out!" Well, well, there's my life, in short,
And so the thing has gone on ever since.
I'm grown a man no doubt, I've broken bounds:
You should not take a fellow eight years old
And make him swear to never kiss the girls.
I'm my own master, paint now as I please—
Having a friend, you see, in the Corner-house!
Lord, it's fast holding by the rings in front—
Those great rings serve more purposes than just
To plant a flag in, or tie up a horse!   230
And yet the old schooling sticks, the old grave eyes
Are peeping o'er my shoulder as I work,
The heads shake still—"It's art's decline, my son!
"You're not of the true painters, great and old;
"Brother Angelico's the man, you'll find;
"Brother Lorenzo stands his single peer:
"Fag on at flesh, you'll never make the third!"

Flower o' the pine,
You keep your mistr ... manners, and I'll stick to mine!
I'm not the third, then: bless us, they must know!   240
Don't you think they're the likeliest to know,
They with their Latin? So, I swallow my rage,
Clench my teeth, suck my lips in tight, and paint
To please them—sometimes do and sometimes don't;
For, doing most, there's pretty sure to come
A turn, some warm eve finds me at my saints—
A laugh, a cry, the business of the world—
(*Flower 'o the peach,*
Death for us all, and his own life for each!)
And my whole soul revolves, the cup runs over,   250
The world and life's too big to pass for a dream,
And I do these wild things in sheer despite,
And play the fooleries you catch me at,
In pure rage! The old mill-horse, out at grass
After hard years, throws up his stiff heels so,
Although the miller does not preach to him
The only good of grass is to make chaff.
What would men have? Do they like grass or no—
May they or mayn't they? all I want's the thing
Settled for ever one way. As it is,   260
You tell too many lies and hurt yourself:
You don't like what you only like too much,
You do like what, if given you at your word,
You find abundantly detestable.
For me, I think I speak as I was taught;
I always see the garden and God there
A-making man's wife: and, my lesson learned,
The value and significance of flesh,
I can't unlearn ten minutes afterwards,

    You understand me: I'm a beast, I know.   270
But see, now—why, I see as certainly

As that the morning-star's about to shine,
What will hap some day. We've a youngster here
Comes to our convent, studies what I do,
Slouches and stares and lets no atom drop:
His name is Guidi—he'll not mind the monks—
They call him Hulking Tom, he lets them talk—
He picks my practice up—he'll paint apace,
I hope so—though I never live so long,
I know what's sure to follow. You be judge!   280
You speak no Latin more than I, belike;
However, you're my man, you've seen the world
—The beauty and the wonder and the power,
The shapes of things, their colours, lights and shades,
Changes, surprises,—and God made it all!
—For what? Do you feel thankful, ay or no,
For this fair town's face, yonder river's line,
The mountain round it and the sky above,
Much more the figures of man, woman, child,
These are the frame to? What's it all about?   290
To be passed over, despised? or dwelt upon,
Wondered at? oh, this last of course!—you say.
But why not do as well as say,—paint these
Just as they are, careless what comes of it?
God's works—paint anyone, and count it crime
To let a truth slip. Don't object, "His works
"Are here already; nature is complete:
"Suppose you reproduce her—(which you can't)
"There's no advantage! you must beat her, then."
For, don't you mark? we're made so that we love   300
First when we see them painted, things we have passed
Perhaps a hundred times nor cared to see;
And so they are better, painted—better to us,
Which is the same thing. Art was given for that;
God uses us to help each other so,
Lending our minds out. Have you noticed, now,

Your cullion's hanging face? A bit of chalk,
And trust me but you should, though! How much
          more,
If I drew higher things with the same truth!
That were to take the Prior's pulpit-place,   310
Interpret God to all of you! Oh, oh,
It makes me mad to see what men shall do
And we in our graves! This world's no blot for us,
Nor blank; it means intensely, and means good:
To find its meaning is my meat and drink.
"Ay, but you don't so instigate to prayer!"
Strikes in the Prior: "when your meaning's plain
"It does not say to folk—remember matins,
"Or, mind you fast next Friday!" Why, for this
What need of art at all? A skull and bones,   320
Two bits of stick nailed crosswise, or, what's best,
A bell to chime the hour with, does as well.
I painted a Saint Laurence six months since
At Prato, splashed the fresco in fine style:
"How looks my painting, now the scaffold's down?"
I ask a brother: "Hugely," he returns—
"Already not one phiz of your three slaves
"Who turn the Deacon off his toasted side,
"But's scratched and prodded to our heart's content,
"The pious people have so eased their own   330
"With coming to say prayers there in a rage:
"We get on fast to see the bricks beneath.
"Expect another job this time next year,
"For pity and religion grow i' the crowd—
"Your painting serves its purpose!" Hang the fools!

    —That is—you'll not mistake an idle word
Spoke in a huff by a poor monk, God wot,
Tasting the air this spicy night which turns
The unaccustomed head like Chianti wine!

Oh, the church knows! don't misreport me, now! 340
It's natural a poor monk out of bounds
Should have his apt word to excuse himself:
And hearken how I plot to make amends.
I have bethought me: I shall paint a piece
... There's for you! Give me six months, then go,
    see
Something in Sant' Ambrogio's! Bless the nuns!
They want a cast o' my office. I shall paint
God in the midst, Madonna and her babe,
Ringed by a bowery flowery angel-brood,
Lilies and vestments and white faces, sweet 350
As puff on puff of grated orris-root
When ladies crowd to Church at midsummer.
And then i' the front, of course a saint or two—
Saint John, because he saves the Florentines,
Saint Ambrose, who puts down in black and white
The convent's friends and gives them a long day,
And Job, I must have him there past mistake,
The man of Uz (and Us without the z,
Painters who need his patience). Well, all these
Secured at their devotion, up shall come 360
Out of a corner when you least expect,
As one by a dark stair into a great light,
Music and talking, who but Lippo! I!—
Mazed, motionless and moonstruck—I'm the man!
Back I shrink—what is this I see and hear?
I, caught up with my monk's-things by mistake,
My old serge gown and rope that goes all round,
I, in this presence, this pure company!
Where's a hole, where's a corner for escape?
Then steps a sweet angelic slip of a thing 370
Forward, puts out a soft palm—"Not so fast!"
—Addresses the celestial presence, "nay—
"He made you and devised you, after all,

"Though he's none of you! Could Saint John there
        draw—
"His camel-hair make up a painting-brush?
"We come to brother Lippo for all that,
"*Iste perfecit opus!*" So, all smile—
I shuffle sideways with my blushing face
Under the cover of a hundred wings
Thrown like a spread of kirtles when you're gay   380
And play hot cockles, all the doors being shut,
Till, wholly unexpected, in there pops
The hothead husband! Thus I scuttle off
To some safe bench behind, not letting go
The palm of her, the little lily thing
That spoke the good word for me in the nick,
Like the Prior's niece . . . Saint Lucy, I would say.
And so all's saved for me, and for the church
A pretty picture gained. Go, six months hence!
Your hand, sir, and good-bye: no lights, no lights!   390
The street's hushed, and I know my own way back,
Don't fear me! There's the grey beginning. Zooks!

ANDREA DEL SARTO.

(CALLED "THE FAULTLESS PAINTER.")

BUT do not let us quarrel any more,
No, my Lucrezia; bear with me for once:
Sit down and all shall happen as you wish.
You turn your face, but does it bring your heart?
I'll work then for your friend's friend, never fear,
Treat his own subject after his own way,
Fix his own time, accept too his own price,
And shut the money into this small hand
When next it takes mine. Will it? tenderly?
Oh, I'll content him,—but to-morrow, Love!   10

Portrait of Francesco Maringhi

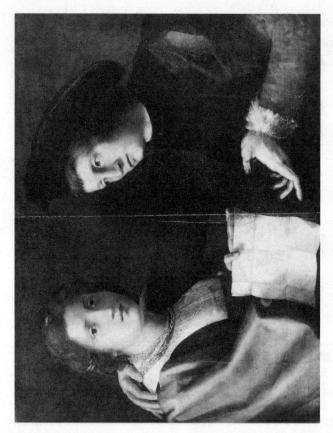

Portrait of the Artist and His Wife

I often am much wearier than you think,
This evening more than usual, and it seems
As if—forgive now—should you let me sit
Here by the window with your hand in mine
And look a half-hour forth on Fiesole,
Both of one mind, as married people use,
Quietly, quietly the evening through,
I might get up to-morrow to my work
Cheerful and fresh as ever. Let us try.
To-morrow, how you shall be glad for this!   20
Your soft hand is a woman of itself,
And mine the man's bared breast she curls inside.
Don't count the time lost, neither; you must serve
For each of the five pictures we require:
It saves a model. So! keep looking so—
My serpentining beauty, rounds on rounds!
—How could you ever prick those perfect ears,
Even to put the pearl there! oh, so sweet—
My face, my moon, my everybody's moon,
Which everybody looks on and calls his,   30
And, I suppose, is looked on by in turn,
While she looks—no one's: very dear, no less.
You smile? why, there's my picture ready made,
There's what we painters call our harmony!
A common greyness silvers everything,—
All in a twilight, you and I alike
—You, at the point of your first pride in me
(That's gone you know),—but I, at every point;
My youth, my hope, my art, being all toned down
To yonder sober pleasant Fiesole.   40
There's the bell clinking from the chapel-top;
That length of convent-wall across the way
Holds the trees safer, huddled more inside;
The last monk leaves the garden; days decrease,
And autumn grows, autumn in everything.
Eh? the whole seems to fall into a shape

As if I saw alike my work and self
And all that I was born to be and do,
A twilight-piece. Love, we are in God's hand.
How strange now, looks the life he makes us lead; 50
So free we seem, so fettered fast we are!
I feel he laid the fetter: let it lie!
This chamber for example—turn your head—
All that's behind us! You don't understand
Nor care to understand about my art,
But you can hear at least when people speak:
And that cartoon, the second from the door
—It is the thing, Love! so such things should be—
Behold Madonna!—I am bold to say.
I can do with my pencil what I know, 60
What I see, what at bottom of my heart
I wish for, if I ever wish so deep—
Do easily, too—when I say, perfectly,
I do not boast, perhaps: yourself are judge,
Who listened to the Legate's talk last week,
And just as much they used to say in France.
At any rate 't is easy, all of it!
No sketches first, no studies, that's long past:
I do what many dream of, all their lives,
—Dream? strive to do, and agonize to do, 70
And fail in doing. I could count twenty such
On twice your fingers, and not leave this town,
Who strive—you don't know how the others strive
To paint a little thing like that you smeared
Carelessly passing with your robes afloat,—
Yet do much less, so much less, Someone says,
(I know his name, no matter)—so much less!
Well, less is more, Lucrezia: I am judged.
There burns a truer light of God in them,
In their vexed beating stuffed and stopped-up brain, 80
Heart, or whate'er else, than goes on to prompt

This low-pulsed forthright craftsman's hand of mine.
Their works drop groundward, but themselves, I know,
Reach many a time a heaven that's shut to me,
Enter and take their place there sure enough,
Though they come back and cannot tell the world.
My works are nearer heaven, but I sit here.
The sudden blood of these men! at a word—
Praise them, it boils, or blame them, it boils too.
I, painting from myself and to myself,   90
Know what I do, am unmoved by men's blame
Or their praise either. Somebody remarks
Morello's outline there is wrongly traced,
His hue mistaken; what of that? or else,
Rightly traced and well ordered; what of that?
Speak as they please, what does the mountain care?
Ah, but a man's reach should exceed his grasp,
Or what's a heaven for? All is silver-grey
Placid and perfect with my art: the worse!
I know both what I want and what might gain,   100
And yet how profitless to know, to sigh
"Had I been two, another and myself,
"Our head would have o'erlooked the world!" No doubt.
Yonder 's a work now, of that famous youth
The Urbinate who died five years ago.
('T is copied, George Vasari sent it me.)
Well, I can fancy how he did it all,
Pouring his soul, with kings and popes to see,
Reaching, that heaven might so replenish him,
Above and through his art—for it gives way;   110
That arm is wrongly put—and there again—
A fault to pardon in the drawing's lines,
Its body, so to speak: its soul is right,
He means right—that, a child may understand.
Still, what an arm! and I could alter it:
But all the play, the insight and the stretch—

Out of me, out of me! And wherefore out?
Had you enjoined them on me, given me soul,
We might have risen to Rafael, I and you!
Nay, Love, you did give all I asked, I think —   120
More than I merit, yes, by many times.
But had you — oh, with the same perfect brow,
And perfect eyes, and more than perfect mouth,
And the low voice my soul hears, as a bird
The fowler's pipe, and follows to the snare —
Had you, with these the same, but brought a mind!
Some women do so. Had the mouth there urged
"God and the glory! never care for gain.
"The present by the future, what is that?
"Live for fame, side by side with Agnolo!   130
"Rafael is waiting: up to God, all three!"
I might have done it for you. So it seems:
Perhaps not. All is as God over-rules.
Beside, incentives come from the soul's self;
The rest avail not. Why do I need you?
What wife had Rafael, or has Agnolo?
In this world, who can do a thing, will not;
And who would do it, cannot, I perceive:
Yet the will's somewhat — somewhat, too, the power —
And thus we half-men struggle. At the end,   140
God, I conclude, compensates, punishes.
'T is safer for me, if the award be strict,
That I am something underrated here,
Poor this long while, despised, to speak the truth.
I dared not, do you know, leave home all day,
For fear of chancing on the Paris lords.
The best is when they pass and look aside;
But they speak sometimes; I must bear it all.
Well may they speak! That Francis, that first time,
And that long festal year at Fontainebleau!   150
I surely then could sometimes leave the ground,

Put on the glory, Rafael's daily wear,
In that humane great monarch's golden look, —
One finger in his beard or twisted curl
Over his mouth's good mark that made the smile,
One arm about my shoulder, round my neck,
The jingle of his gold chain in my ear,
I painting proudly with his breath on me,
All his court round him, seeing with his eyes,
Such frank French eyes, and such a fire of souls   160
Profuse, my hand kept plying by those hearts, —
And, best of all, this, this, this face beyond,
This in the background, waiting on my work,
To crown the issue with a last reward!
A good time, was it not, my kingly days?
And had you not grown restless ... but I know —
'T is done and past; 't was right, my instinct said;
Too live the life grew, golden and not grey,
And I'm the weak-eyed bat no sun should tempt
Out of the grange whose four walls make his world.   170
How could it end in any other way?
You called me, and I came home to your heart.
The triumph was — to reach and stay there; since
I reached it ere the triumph, what is lost?
Let my hands frame your face in your hair's gold,
You beautiful Lucrezia that are mine!
"Rafael did this, Andrea painted that;
"The Roman's is the better when you pray,
"But still the other's Virgin was his wife —"
Men will excuse me. I am glad to judge   180
Both pictures in your presence; clearer grows
My better fortune, I resolve to think.
For, do you know, Lucrezia, as God lives,
Said one day Agnolo, his very self,
To Rafael ... I have known it all these years ...
(When the young man was flaming out his thoughts

Upon a palace-wall for Rome to see,
Too lifted up in heart because of it)
"Friend, there's a certain sorry little scrub
"Goes up and down our Florence, none cares how,   190
"Who, were he set to plan and execute
"As you are, pricked on by your popes and kings,
"Would bring the sweat into that brow of yours!"
To Rafael's!—And indeed the arm is wrong.
I hardly dare ... yet, only you to see,
Give the chalk here—quick, thus the line should go!
Ay, but the soul! he's Rafael! rub it out!
Still, all I care for, if he spoke the truth,
(What he? why, who but Michel Agnolo?
Do you forget already words like those?)   200
If really there was such a chance, so lost,—
Is, whether you're—not grateful—but more pleased.
Well, let me think so. And you smile indeed!
This hour has been an hour! Another smile?
If you would sit thus by me every night
I should work better, do you comprehend?
I mean that I should earn more, give you more.
See, it is settled dusk now; there's a star;
Morello's gone, the watch-lights show the wall,
The cue-owls speak the name we call them by.   210
Come from the window, love,—come in, at last,
Inside the melancholy little house
We built to be so gay with. God is just.
King Francis may forgive me: oft at nights
When I look up from painting, eyes tired out,
The walls become illumined, brick from brick
Distinct, instead of mortar, fierce bright gold,
That gold of his I did cement them with!
Let us but love each other. Must you go?
That Cousin here again? he waits outside?   220
Must see you—you, and not with me? Those loans?

More gaming debts to pay? you smiled for that?
Well, let smiles buy me! have you more to spend?
While hand and eye and something of a heart
Are left me, work's my ware, and what's it worth?
I'll pay my fancy. Only let me sit
The grey remainder of the evening out,
Idle, you call it, and muse perfectly
How I could paint, were I but back in France,
One picture, just one more—the Virgin's face,   230
Not yours this time! I want you at my side
To hear them—that is, Michel Agnolo—
Judge all I do and tell you of its worth.
Will you? To-morrow, satisfy your friend.
I take the subjects for his corridor,
Finish the portrait out of hand—there, there,
And throw him in another thing or two
If he demurs; the whole should prove enough
To pay for this same Cousin's freak. Beside,
What's better and what's all I care about,   240
Get you the thirteen scudi for the ruff!
Love, does that please you? Ah, but what does he,
The Cousin! what does he to please you more?

    I am grown peaceful as old age to-night.
I regret little, I would change still less.
Since there my past life lies, why alter it?
The very wrong to Francis!—it is true
I took his coin, was tempted and complied,
And built this house and sinned, and all is said.
My father and my mother died of want.   250
Well, had I riches of my own? you see
How one gets rich! Let each one bear his lot.
They were born poor, lived poor, and poor they died:
And I have laboured somewhat in my time
And not been paid profusely. Some good son

Paint my two hundred pictures—let him try!
No doubt, there's something strikes a balance. Yes,
You loved me quite enough, it seems to-night.
This must suffice me here. What would one have?
In heaven, perhaps, new chances, one more chance—　　260
Four great walls in the New Jerusalem,
Meted on each side by the angel's reed,
For Leonard, Rafael, Agnolo and me
To cover—the three first without a wife,
While I have mine! So—still they overcome
Because there's still Lucrezia,—as I choose.

Again the Cousin's whistle! Go, my Love.

A GRAMMARIAN'S FUNERAL,

SHORTLY AFTER THE REVIVAL OF LEARNING IN EUROPE.

LET us begin and carry up this corpse,
　　　Singing together.
Leave we the common crofts, the vulgar thorpes
　　　Each in its tether
Sleeping safe on the bosom of the plain,
　　　Cared-for till cock-crow:
Look out if yonder be not day again
　　　Rimming the rock-row!
That's the appropriate country; there, man's thought,
　　　Rarer, intenser,　　　　　　　　　　　　　　10
Self-gathered for an outbreak, as it ought,
　　　Chafes in the censer.
Leave we the unlettered plain its herd and crop;
　　　Seek we sepulture
On a tall mountain, citied to the top,
　　　Crowded with culture!

All the peaks soar, but one the rest excels;
      Clouds overcome it;
No! yonder sparkle is the citadel's
      Circling its summit.   20
Thither our path lies; wind we up the heights:
      Wait ye the warning?
Our low life was the level's and the night's;
      He's for the morning.
Step to a tune, square chests, erect each head,
      'Ware the beholders!
This is our master, famous calm and dead,
      Borne on our shoulders.

Sleep, crop and herd! sleep, darkling thorpe and croft,
      Safe from the weather!   30
He, whom we convoy to his grave aloft,
      Singing together,
He was a man born with thy face and throat,
      Lyric Apollo!
Long he lived nameless: how should spring take note
      Winter would follow?
Till lo, the little touch, and youth was gone!
      Cramped and diminished,
Moaned he, "New measures, other feet anon!
      "My dance is finished?"   40
No, that's the world's way: (keep the mountain-side,
      Make for the city!)
He knew the signal, and stepped on with pride
      Over men's pity;
Left play for work, and grappled with the world
      Bent on escaping:
"What's in the scroll," quoth he, "thou keepest furled?
      "Show me their shaping,
"Theirs who most studied man, the bard and sage, —
      "Give!" — So, he gowned him,   50

Straight got by heart that book to its last page:
     Learned, we found him.
Yea, but we found him bald too, eyes like lead,
     Accents uncertain:
"Time to taste life," another would have said,
     "Up with the curtain!"
This man said rather, "Actual life comes next?
     "Patience a moment!
"Grant I have mastered learning's crabbed text,
     "Still there's the comment.   60
"Let me know all! Prate not of most or least,
     "Painful or easy!
"Even to the crumbs I'd fain eat up the feast,
     "Ay, nor feel queasy."
Oh, such a life as he resolved to live,
     When he had learned it,
When he had gathered all books had to give!
     Sooner, he spurned it.
Image the whole, then execute the parts—
     Fancy the fabric   70
Quite, ere you build, ere steel strike fire from quartz,
     Ere mortar dab brick!

(Here's the town-gate reached: there's the market-place
     Gaping before us.)
Yea, this in him was the peculiar grace
     (Hearten our chorus!)
That before living he'd learn how to live—
     No end to learning:
Earn the means first—God surely will contrive
     Use for our earning.   80
Others mistrust and say, "But time escapes:
     "Live now or never!"
He said, "What's time? Leave Now for dogs and
         apes!
     "Man has Forever."

Back to his book then: deeper drooped his head:
    Calculus racked him:
Leaden before, his eyes grew dross of lead:
    Tussis attacked him.
"Now, master, take a little rest!"—not he!
    (Caution redoubled,   90
Step two abreast, the way winds narrowly!)
    Not a whit troubled
Back to his studies, fresher than at first,
    Fierce as a dragon
He (soul-hydroptic with a sacred thirst)
    Sucked at the flagon.
Oh, if we draw a circle premature,
    Heedless of far gain,
Greedy for quick returns of profit, sure
    Bad is our bargain!   100
Was it not great? did not he throw on God,
    (He loves the burthen)—
God's task to make the heavenly period
    Perfect the earthen?
Did not he magnify the mind, show clear
    Just what it all meant?
He would not discount life, as fools do here,
    Paid by instalment.
He ventured neck or nothing—heaven's success
    Found, or earth's failure: 110
"Wilt thou trust death or not?" He answered "Yes:
    "Hence with life's pale lure!"
That low man seeks a little thing to do,
    Sees it and does it:
This high man, with a great thing to pursue,
    Dies ere he knows it.
That low man goes on adding one to one,
    His hundred's soon hit:
This high man, aiming at a million,
    Misses an unit.   120

That, has the world here—should he need the next,
      Let the world mind him!
This, throws himself on God, and unperplexed
      Seeking shall find him.
So, with the throttling hands of death at strife,
      Ground he at grammar;
Still, thro' the rattle, parts of speech were rife:
      While he could stammer
He settled *Hoti's* business—let it be!—
      Properly based *Oun*—   130
Gave us the doctrine of the enclitic *De*,
      Dead from the waist down.
Well, here's the platform, here's the proper place:
      Hail to your purlieus,
All ye highfliers of the feathered race,
      Swallows and curlews!
Here's the top-peak; the multitude below
      Live, for they can, there:
This man decided not to Live but Know—
      Bury this man there?   140
Here—here's his place, where meteors shoot, clouds
        form,
      Lightnings are loosened,
Stars come and go! Let joy break with the storm,
      Peace let the dew send!
Lofty designs must close in like effects:
      Loftily lying,
Leave him—still loftier than the world suspects,
      Living and dying.

"IMPERANTE AUGUSTO NATUS EST—"

WHAT it was struck the terror into me?
This, Publius: closer! while we wait our turn
I'll tell you. Water's warm (they ring inside)
At the eighth hour, till when no use to bathe.

Here in the vestibule where now we sit,
One scarce stood yesterday, the throng was such
Of loyal gapers, folk all eye and ear
While Lucius Varius Rufus in their midst
Read out that long-planned late-completed piece,
His Panegyric on the Emperor.   10
"Nobody like him" little Flaccus laughed
"At leading forth an Epos with due pomp!
Only, when godlike Cæsar swells the theme,
How should mere mortals hope to praise aright?
Tell me, thou offshoot of Etruscan kings!"
Whereat Mæcenas smiling sighed assent.

I paid my quadrans, left the Thermæ's roar
Of rapture as the poet asked "What place
Among the godships Jove, for Cæsar's sake,
Would bid its actual occupant vacate   20
In favour of the new divinity?"
And got the expected answer "Yield thine own!"—
Jove thus dethroned, I somehow wanted air,
And found myself a-pacing street and street,
Letting the sunset, rosy over Rome,
Clear my head dizzy with the hubbub—say,
As if thought's dance therein had kicked up dust
By trampling on all else: the world lay prone,
As—poet-propped, in brave hexameters—

Their subject triumphed up from man to God.   30
Caius Octavius Cæsar the August—
Where was escape from his prepotency?
I judge I may have passed—how many piles
Of structure dropt like doles from his free hand
To Rome on every side? Why, right and left,
For temples you've the Thundering Jupiter,
Avenging Mars, Apollo Palatine:
How count Piazza, Forum—there's a third
All but completed. You've the Theatre
Named of Marcellus—all his work, such work!—   40
One thought still ending, dominating all—
With warrant Varius sang "Be Cæsar God!"
By what a hold arrests he Fortune's wheel,
Obtaining and retaining heaven and earth
Through Fortune, if you like, but favour—no!
For the great deeds flashed by me, fast and thick
As stars which storm the sky on autumn nights—
Those conquests! but peace crowned them,—so, of peace!
Count up his titles only—these, in few—
Ten years Triumvir, Consul thirteen times,   50
Emperor, nay—the glory topping all—
Hailed Father of his Country, last and best
Of titles, by himself accepted so:
And why not? See but feats achieved in Rome—
Not to say, Italy—he planted there
Some thirty colonies—but Rome itself
All new-built, "marble now, brick once," he boasts:
This Portico, that Circus. Would you sail?
He has drained Tiber for you: would you walk?
He straightened out the long Flaminian Way.   60
Poor? Profit by his score of donatives!
Rich—that is, mirthful? Half-a-hundred games
Challenge your choice! There's Rome—for you and me
Only? The centre of the world besides!

For, look the wide world over, where ends Rome?
To sunrise? There's Euphrates—all between!
To sunset? Ocean and immensity:
North,—stare till Danube stops you: South, see Nile,
The Desert and the earth-upholding Mount.
Well may the poet-people each with each   70
Vie in his praise, our company of swans,
Virgil and Horace, singers—in their way—
Nearly as good as Varius, though less famed:
Well may they cry, "No mortal, plainly God!"

Thus to myself said, while I walked:
Or would have said, could thought attain to speech,
Clean baffled by enormity of bliss
The while I strove to scale its heights and sound
Its depths—this masterdom o'er all the world
Of one who was but born,—like you, like me,   80
Like all the world he owns,—of flesh and blood.
But he—how grasp, how gauge his own conceit
Of bliss to me near inconceivable?
Or—since such flight too much makes reel the brain—
Let's sink—and so take refuge, as it were,
From life's excessive altitude—to life's
Breathable wayside shelter at its base!
If looms thus large this Cæsar to myself
—Of senatorial rank and somebody—
How must he strike the vulgar nameless crowd,   90
Innumerous swarm that's nobody at all?
Why,—for an instance,—much as yon gold shape
Crowned, sceptred, on the temple opposite—
Fulgurant Jupiter—must daze the sense
Of—say, yon outcast begging from its step!
What, anti-Cæsar, monarch in the mud,
As he is pinnacled above thy pate?
Ay, beg away! thy lot contrasts full well

With his whose bounty yields thee this support—
Our Holy and Inviolable One,   100
Cæsar, whose bounty built the fane above!
Dost read my thought? Thy garb, alack, displays
Sore usage truly in each rent and stain—
Faugh! Wash though in Suburra! 'Ware the dogs
Who may not so disdain a meal on thee!
What, stretchest forth a palm to catch my alms?
Aha, why yes: I must appear—who knows?—
I, in my toga, to thy rags and thee—
Quæstor—nay, Ædile, Censor—Pol! perhaps
The very City-Prætor's noble self!   110
As to me Cæsar, so to thee am I?
Good: nor in vain shall prove thy quest, poor rogue!
Hither—hold palm out—take this quarter-as!

And who did take it? As he raised his head,
(My gesture was a trifle—well, abrupt),
Back fell the broad flap of the peasant's-hat,
The homespun cloak that muffled half his cheek
Dropped somewhat, and I had a glimpse—just one!
One was enough. Whose—whose might be the face?
That unkempt careless hair—brown, yellowish—   120
Those sparkling eyes beneath their eyebrows' ridge
(Each meets each, and the hawk-nose rules between)
—That was enough, no glimpse was needed more!
And terrifyingly into my mind
Came that quick-hushed report was whispered us,
"They do say, once a year in sordid garb
He plays the mendicant, sits all day long,
Asking and taking alms of who may pass,
And so averting, if submission help,
Fate's envy, the dread chance and change of things   130
When Fortune—for a word, a look, a nought—
Turns spiteful and—the petted lioness—

Strikes with her sudden paw, and prone falls each
Who patted late her neck superiorly,
Or trifled with those claw-tips velvet-sheathed."
"He's God!" shouts Lucius Varius Rufus: "Man
And worms'-meat any moment!" mutters low
Some Power, admonishing the mortal-born.

Ay, do you mind? There's meaning in the fact
That whoso conquers, triumphs, enters Rome,   140
Climbing the Capitolian, soaring thus
To glory's summit,—Publius, do you mark—
Ever the same attendant who, behind,
Above the Conqueror's head supports the crown
All-too-demonstrative for human wear,
—One hand's employment—all the while reserves
Its fellow, backward flung, to point how, close
Appended from the car, beneath the foot
Of the up-borne exulting Conqueror,
Frown—half-descried—the instruments of shame,   150
The malefactor's due. Crown, now—Cross, when?

Who stands secure? Are even Gods so safe?
Jupiter that just now is dominant—
Are not there ancient dismal tales how once
A predecessor reigned ere Saturn came,
And who can say if Jupiter be last?
Was it for nothing the grey Sibyl wrote
"Cæsar Augustus regnant, shall be born
In blind Judæa"—one to master him,
Him and the universe? An old-wife's tale?   160

Bath-drudge! Here, slave! No cheating! Our turn next.
No loitering, or be sure you taste the lash!
Two strigils, two oil-drippers, each a sponge!

UP AT A VILLA—DOWN IN THE CITY.

(AS DISTINGUISHED BY AN ITALIAN PERSON
OF QUALITY.)

I.

HAD I but plenty of money, money enough and to spare,
The house for me, no doubt, were a house in the city-
    square;
Ah, such a life, such a life, as one leads at the window
    there!

II.

Something to see, by Bacchus, something to hear, at
    least!
There, the whole day long, one's life is a perfect feast;
While up at a villa one lives, I maintain it, no more than
    a beast.

III.

Well now, look at our villa! stuck like the horn of a bull
Just on a mountain-edge as bare as the creature's skull,
Save a mere shag of a bush with hardly a leaf to pull!
—I scratch my own, sometimes, to see if the hair's
    turned wool.   10

IV.

But the city, oh the city—the square with the houses!
    Why?
They are stone-faced, white as a curd, there's something
    to take the eye!

Houses in four straight lines, not a single front awry;
You watch who crosses and gossips, who saunters, who
   hurries by;
Green blinds, as a matter of course, to draw when the
   sun gets high;
And the shops with fanciful signs which are painted
   properly.

V.

What of a villa? Though winter be over in March by
   rights,
'T is May perhaps ere the snow shall have withered well
   off the heights:
You've the brown ploughed land before, where the oxen
   steam and wheeze,
And the hills over-smoked behind by the faint grey olive-
   trees.   20

VI.

Is it better in May, I ask you? You've summer all at once;
In a day he leaps complete with a few strong April suns.
'Mid the sharp short emerald wheat, scarce risen three
   fingers well,
The wild tulip, at end of its tube, blows out its great red
   bell
Like a thin clear bubble of blood, for the children to pick
   and sell.

VII.

Is it ever hot in the square? There's a fountain to spout
   and splash!
In the shade it sings and springs; in the shine such foam-
   bows flash

On the horses with curling fish-tails, that prance and
    paddle and pash
Round the lady atop in her conch—fifty gazers do not
    abash,
Though all that she wears is some weeds round her waist
    in a sort of sash.   30

VIII.

All the year long at the villa, nothing to see though you
    linger,
Except yon cypress that points like death's lean lifted
    forefinger.
Some think fireflies pretty, when they mix i' the corn and
    mingle,
Or thrid the stinking hemp till the stalks of it seem
    a-tingle.
Late August or early September, the stunning cicala is
    shrill,
And the bees keep their tiresome whine round the resin-
    ous firs on the hill.
Enough of the seasons,—I spare you the months of the
    fever and chill.

IX.

Ere you open your eyes in the city, the blessed church-
    bells begin:
No sooner the bells leave off than the diligence rattles
    in:
You get the pick of the news, and it costs you never a
    pin.   40
By-and-by there's the travelling doctor gives pills, lets
    blood, draws teeth;
Or the Pulcinello-trumpet breaks up the market beneath.
At the post-office such a scene-picture—the new play,
    piping hot!

And a notice how, only this morning, three liberal
    thieves were shot.
Above it, behold the Archbishop's most fatherly of re-
    bukes,
And beneath, with his crown and his lion, some little
    new law of the Duke's!
Or a sonnet with flowery marge, to the Reverend Don
    So-and-so
Who is Dante, Boccaccio, Petrarca, Saint Jerome and
    Cicero,
"And moreover," (the sonnet goes rhyming,) "the skirts
    of Saint Paul has reached,
"Having preached us those six Lent-lectures more unc-
    tuous than ever he preached."   50
Noon strikes,—here sweeps the procession! our Lady
    borne smiling and smart
With a pink gauze gown all spangles, and seven swords
    stuck in her heart!
Bang-whang-whang goes the drum, *tootle-te-tootle* the fife;
No keeping one's haunches still: it's the greatest pleasure
    in life.

X.

But bless you, it's dear—it's dear! fowls, wine, at double
    the rate.
They have clapped a new tax upon salt, and what oil pays
    passing the gate
It's a horror to think of. And so, the villa for me, not the
    city!
Beggars can scarcely be choosers: but still—ah, the pity,
    the pity!
Look, two and two go the priests, then the monks with
    cowls and sandals,
And the penitents dressed in white shirts, a-holding the
    yellow candles;   60

One, he carries a flag up straight, and another a cross
    with handles,
And the Duke's guard brings up the rear, for the better
    prevention of scandals:
Bang-whang-whang goes the drum, *tootle-te-tootle* the fife.
Oh, a day in the city-square, there is no such pleasure in
    life!

"*CHILDE ROLAND TO THE DARK TOWER CAME.*"

(See Edgar's song in "LEAR.")

I.

MY first thought was, he lied in every word,
    That hoary cripple, with malicious eye
    Askance to watch the working of his lie
On mine, and mouth scarce able to afford
Suppression of the glee, that pursed and scored
    Its edge, at one more victim gained thereby.

II.

What else should he be set for, with his staff?
    What, save to waylay with his lies, ensnare
    All travellers who might find him posted there,
And ask the road? I guessed what skull-like laugh   10
Would break, what crutch 'gin write my epitaph
    For pastime in the dusty thoroughfare,

III.

If at his counsel I should turn aside
    Into that ominous tract which, all agree,
    Hides the Dark Tower. Yet acquiescingly

I did turn as he pointed: neither pride
Nor hope rekindling at the end descried,
   So much as gladness that some end might be.

IV.

For, what with my whole world-wide wandering,
   What with my search drawn out thro' years, my
       hope   20
   Dwindled into a ghost not fit to cope
With that obstreperous joy success would bring, —
I hardly tried now to rebuke the spring
   My heart made, finding failure in its scope.

V.

As when a sick man very near to death
   Seems dead indeed, and feels begin and end
   The tears and takes the farewell of each friend,
And hears one bid the other go, draw breath
Freelier outside, ("since all is o'er," he saith,
   "And the blow fallen no grieving can amend;")   30

VI.

While some discuss if near the other graves
   Be room enough for this, and when a day
   Suits best for carrying the corpse away,
With care about the banners, scarves and staves:
And still the man hears all, and only craves
   He may not shame such tender love and stay.

VII.

Thus, I had so long suffered in this quest,
   Heard failure prophesied so oft, been writ

So many times among "The Band"—to wit,
The knights who to the Dark Tower's search
          addressed   40
Their steps—that just to fail as they, seemed best,
  And all the doubt was now—should I be fit?

VIII.

So, quiet as despair, I turned from him,
  That hateful cripple, out of his highway
  Into the path he pointed. All the day
Had been a dreary one at best, and dim
Was settling to its close, yet shot one grim
  Red leer to see the plain catch its estray.

IX.

For mark! no sooner was I fairly found
  Pledged to the plain, after a pace or two,   50
  Than, pausing to throw backward a last view
O'er the safe road, 't was gone; grey plain all round:
Nothing but plain to the horizon's bound.
  I might go on; nought else remained to do.

X.

So, on I went. I think I never saw
  Such starved ignoble nature; nothing throve:
  For flowers—as well expect a cedar grove!
But cockle, spurge, according to their law
Might propagate their kind, with none to awe,
  You'd think; a burr had been a treasure-trove.   60

XI.

No! penury, inertness and grimace,
  In some strange sort, were the land's portion. "See

"Or shut your eyes," said Nature peevishly,
"It nothing skills: I cannot help my case:
"'T is the Last Judgment's fire must cure this place,
"Calcine its clods and set my prisoners free."

XII.

If there pushed any ragged thistle-stalk
  Above its mates, the head was chopped; the bents
  Were jealous else. What made those holes and rents
In the dock's harsh swarth leaves, bruised as to baulk   70
All hope of greenness? 't is a brute must walk
  Pashing their life out, with a brute's intents.

XIII.

As for the grass, it grew as scant as hair
  In leprosy; thin dry blades pricked the mud
  Which underneath looked kneaded up with blood.
One stiff blind horse, his every bone a-stare,
Stood stupefied, however he came there:
  Thrust out past service from the devil's stud!

XIV.

Alive? he might be dead for aught I know,
  With that red gaunt and colloped neck a-strain,   80
  And shut eyes underneath the rusty mane;
Seldom went such grotesqueness with such woe;
I never saw a brute I hated so;
  He must be wicked to deserve such pain.

XV.

I shut my eyes and turned them on my heart.
  As a man calls for wine before he fights,

I asked one draught of earlier, happier sights,
Ere fitly I could hope to play my part.
Think first, fight afterwards—the soldier's art:
   One taste of the old time sets all to rights.   90

XVI.

Not it! I fancied Cuthbert's reddening face
   Beneath its garniture of curly gold,
   Dear fellow, till I almost felt him fold
An arm in mine to fix me to the place,
That way he used. Alas, one night's disgrace!
   Out went my heart's new fire and left it cold.

XVII.

Giles then, the soul of honour—there he stands
   Frank as ten years ago when knighted first.
   What honest man should dare (he said) he durst.
Good—but the scene shifts—faugh! what hangman-
            hands   100
Pin to his breast a parchment? His own bands
   Read it. Poor traitor, spit upon and curst!

XVIII.

Better this present than a past like that;
   Back therefore to my darkening path again!
   No sound, no sight as far as eye could strain.
Will the night send a howlet or a bat?
I asked: when something on the dismal flat
   Came to arrest my thoughts and change their train.

XIX.

A sudden little river crossed my path
   As unexpected as a serpent comes.   110

Hermes and Apollo

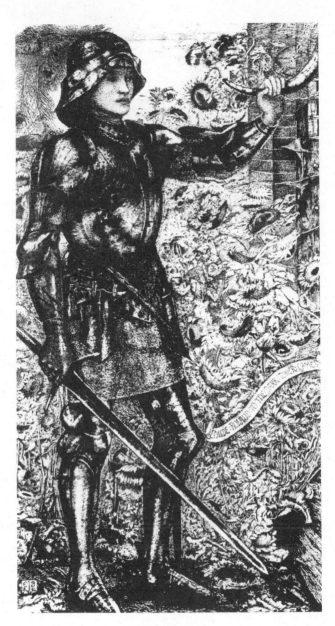

Childe Roland

No sluggish tide congenial to the glooms;
This, as it frothed by, might have been a bath
For the fiend's glowing hoof—to see the wrath
    Of its black eddy bespate with flakes and spumes.

XX.

So petty yet so spiteful! All along,
    Low scrubby alders kneeled down over it;
    Drenched willows flung them headlong in a fit
Of mute despair, a suicidal throng:
The river which had done them all the wrong,
    Whate'er that was, rolled by, deterred no whit.   120

XXI.

Which, while I forded,—good saints, how I feared
    To set my foot upon a dead man's cheek,
    Each step, or feel the spear I thrust to seek
For hollows, tangled in his hair or beard!
—It may have been a water-rat I speared,
    But, ugh! it sounded like a baby's shriek.

XXII.

Glad was I when I reached the other bank.
    Now for a better country. Vain presage!
    Who were the strugglers, what war did they wage,
Whose savage trample thus could pad the dank   130
Soil to a plash? Toads in a poisoned tank,
    Or wild cats in a red-hot iron cage—

XXIII.

The fight must so have seemed in that fell cirque.
    What penned them there, with all the plain to choose?
    No foot-print leading to that horrid mews,

None out of it. Mad brewage set to work
Their brains, no doubt, like galley-slaves the Turk
  Pits for his pastime, Christians against Jews.

XXIV.

And more than that—a furlong on—why, there!
  What bad use was that engine for, that wheel,   140
  Or brake, not wheel—that harrow fit to reel
Men's bodies out like silk? with all the air
Of Tophet's tool, on earth left unaware,
  Or brought to sharpen its rusty teeth of steel.

XXV.

Then came a bit of stubbed ground, once a wood,
  Next a marsh, it would seem, and now mere earth
  Desperate and done with; (so a fool finds mirth,
Makes a thing and then mars it, till his mood
Changes and off he goes!) within a rood—
  Bog, clay and rubble, sand and stark black dearth.   150

XXVI.

Now blotches rankling, coloured gay and grim,
  Now patches where some leanness of the soil's
  Broke into moss or substances like boils;
Then came some palsied oak, a cleft in him
Like a distorted mouth that splits its rim
  Gaping at death, and dies while it recoils.

XXVII.

And just as far as ever from the end!
  Nought in the distance but the evening, nought
  To point my footstep further! At the thought,

A great black bird, Apollyon's bosom-friend,   160
Sailed past, nor beat his wide wing dragon-penned
   That brushed my cap—perchance the guide I sought.

XXVIII.

For, looking up, aware I somehow grew,
   'Spite of the dusk, the plain had given place
   All round to mountains—with such name to grace
Mere ugly heights and heaps now stolen in view.
How thus they had surprised me,—solve it, you!
   How to get from them was no clearer case.

XXIX.

Yet half I seemed to recognize some trick
   Of mischief happened to me, God knows when—   170
   In a bad dream perhaps. Here ended, then,
Progress this way. When, in the very nick
Of giving up, one time more, came a click
   As when a trap shuts—you're inside the den!

XXX.

Burningly it came on me all at once,
   This was the place! those two hills on the right,
   Crouched like two bulls locked horn in horn in fight;
While to the left, a tall scalped mountain . . . Dunce,
Dotard, a-dozing at the very nonce,
   After a life spent training for the sight!   180

XXXI.

What in the midst lay but the Tower itself?
   The round squat turret, blind as the fool's heart,
   Built of brown stone, without a counterpart

In the whole world. The tempest's mocking elf
Points to the shipman thus the unseen shelf
   He strikes on, only when the timbers start.

XXXII.

Not see? because of night perhaps?—why, day
   Came back again for that! before it left,
   The dying sunset kindled through a cleft:
The hills, like giants at a hunting, lay,   190
Chin upon hand, to see the game at bay, —
   "Now stab and end the creature—to the heft!

XXXIII.

Not hear? when noise was everywhere! it tolled
   Increasing like a bell. Names in my ears
   Of all the lost adventurers my peers, —
How such a one was strong, and such was bold,
And such was fortunate, yet each of old
   Lost, lost! one moment knelled the woe of years.

XXXIV.

There they stood, ranged along the hill-sides, met
   To view the last of me, a living frame   200
   For one more picture! in a sheet of flame
I saw them and I knew them all. And yet
Dauntless the slug-horn to my lips I set,
   And blew. "*Childe Roland to the Dark Tower came.*"

PERSONAL POEMS

BROWNING GUARDED HIS private life from his readers. Although his poems reflect his own concerns and interests, he was careful to separate the poet from the man. He seldom speaks in his own voice and, when he does, it is cautious and admonitory. In the late poem "House," for example, he specifically warns his readers not to expect personal revelations in his poetry.

Yet, for all his reticence, it is clear that Browning's poetry is less detached than was once believed. Like the poet in "How it Strikes a Contemporary" Browning did not live a flamboyant or extravagant private life. Only on one occasion, in his clandestine marriage to Elizabeth Barrett, did he flout society's conventions. Yet his outwardly uneventful life possessed an emotional richness which he was unable or unwilling to suppress entirely in his writing.

The poems in this final section all give glimpses of Browning the man. They begin with him as a young boy at home in the cottage in Camberwell with his pony and dogs. His scholarly father who worked as a clerk in the Bank of England is teaching him Greek in simple stages. Several years later Browning's enthusiasm for the poet Shelley is shown in "Memorabilia." This poem portrays the spontaneity and excitability of the young Browning, an intensity which frequently made him appear gauche in company, but which endeared him to his friends.

133

Among these early friends was Alfred Domett, who lived near the Brownings and with Robert was a member of the Colloquials, a small group of like-minded young men who met regularly to discuss poetry and other literary topics. In the early 1840's Domett emigrated to New Zealand where he later became Prime Minister. Browning never forgot him. Their friendship is shown in "The Guardian-Angel," which Browning wrote after an 1848 visit—with his wife—to Fano in Italy. In addressing the poem to Domett, Browning metaphorically introduced his absent friend to Elizabeth.

Elizabeth Barrett Browning herself is the subject of a number of poems. Chief among these is "By the Fire-side," a poem in which Browning describes a scene which occurred soon after their marriage, when they were on holiday at Bagni di Lucca in 1849. Their love for each other had been deepened by the recent birth of their son, and, in a moment of intense happiness, they achieved an intuitive mutual understanding. Many of the incidental details of this poem are accurate, but in other autobiographical poems the central emotional truth is clothed in a fictional setting.

Elizabeth's death in 1861 brought forth "Prospice," one of Browning's strongest affirmations of his Christian belief. He still had another twenty-eight years to live, years in which Elizabeth's memory inspired, challenged and frustrated him. "O lyric Love," an extract from *The Ring and the Book*, shows how Elizabeth's spiritual presence sustained Browning in his task of writing poetry. "Never the Time and the Place" shows a temporary doubt, as Browning, frustrated and lonely by the loss of Elizabeth, questions whether they will ever be spiritually reunited. Other poems of the 1870's and early 1880's display moments of guilt when Browning feels he may have betrayed Elizabeth's memory.

The final poem in the section, the epilogue to Browning's last work *Asolando*, is addressed to another friend, the American Katharine Bronson, whom Browning had met in Venice.

Written in the last months of his life, the poem anticipates Browning's death and attempts to summarize his thoughts on who and what he has been. His sister Sarianna thought it gloomy and full of foreboding. He himself at first believed it rather boastful, but, after more thought, said, "It's the simple truth, and as it is true, it shall stand."

HOUSE.

I.

SHALL I sonnet-sing you about myself?
  Do I live in a house you would like to see?
Is it scant of gear, has it store of pelf?
  "Unlock my heart with a sonnet-key?"

II.

Invite the world, as my betters have done?
  "Take notice: this building remains on view,
Its suites of reception every one,
  Its private apartment and bedroom too;

III.

"For a ticket, apply to the Publisher."
  No: thanking the public, I must decline.   10
A peep through my window, if folk prefer;
  But, please you, no foot over threshold of mine!

IV.

I have mixed with a crowd and heard free talk
  In a foreign land where an earthquake chanced:

And a house stood gaping, nought to baulk
   Man's eye wherever he gazed or glanced.

V.

The whole of the frontage shaven sheer,
   The inside gaped: exposed to day,
Right and wrong and common and queer,
   Bare, as the palm of your hand, it lay.   20

VI.

The owner? Oh, he had been crushed, no doubt!
   "Odd tables and chairs for a man of wealth!
What a parcel of musty old books about!
   He smoked, —no wonder he lost his health!

VII.

"I doubt if he bathed before he dressed.
   A brasier?—the pagan, he burned perfumes!
You see it is proved, what the neighbours guessed:
   His wife and himself had separate rooms."

VIII.

Friends, the goodman of the house at least
   Kept house to himself till an earthquake came: 30
'T is the fall of its frontage permits you feast
   On the inside arrangement you praise or blame.

IX.

Outside should suffice for evidence:
   And whoso desires to penetrate

Deeper, must dive by the spirit-sense–
   No optics like yours, at any rate!

                    x.

"Hoity toity! A street to explore,
   Your house the exception! '*With this same key*
Shakespeare unlocked his heart,' once more!"
      Did Shakespeare? If so, the less Shakespeare he!   40

HOW IT STRIKES A CONTEMPORARY.

I ONLY knew one poet in my life:
And this, or something like it, was his way.

   You saw go up and down Valladolid,
A man of mark, to know next time you saw.
His very serviceable suit of black
Was courtly once and conscientious still,
And many might have worn it, though none did:
The cloak, that somewhat shone and showed the threads,
Had purpose, and the ruff, significance.
He walked and tapped the pavement with his cane,   10
Scenting the world, looking it full in face,
An old dog, bald and blindish, at his heels.
They turned up, now, the alley by the church,
That leads nowhither; now, they breathed themselves
On the main promenade just at the wrong time:
You'd come upon his scrutinizing hat,
Making a peaked shade blacker than itself
Against the single window spared some house
Intact yet with its mouldered Moorish work, —
Or else surprise the ferrel of his stick   20

Trying the mortar's temper 'tween the chinks
Of some new shop a-building, French and fine.
He stood and watched the cobbler at his trade,
The man who slices lemons into drink,
The coffee-roaster's brazier, and the boys
That volunteer to help him turn its winch.
He glanced o'er books on stalls with half an eye,
And fly-leaf ballads on the vendor's string,
And broad-edge bold-print posters by the wall.
He took such cognizance of men and things,   30
If any beat a horse, you felt he saw;
If any cursed a woman, he took note;
Yet stared at nobody,—you stared at him,
And found, less to your pleasure than surprise,
He seemed to know you and expect as much.
So, next time that a neighbour's tongue was loosed,
It marked the shameful and notorious fact,
We had among us, not so much a spy,
As a recording chief-inquisitor,
The town's true master if the town but knew!   40
We merely kept a governor for form,
While this man walked about and took account
Of all thought, said and acted, then went home,
And wrote it fully to our Lord the King
Who has an itch to know things, he knows why,
And reads them in his bedroom of a night.
Oh, you might smile! there wanted not a touch,
A tang of . . . well, it was not wholly ease
As back into your mind the man's look came.
Stricken in years a little,—such a brow   50
His eyes had to live under!—clear as flint
On either side the formidable nose
Curved, cut and coloured like an eagle's claw.
Had he to do with A.'s surprising fate?
When altogether old B. disappeared
And young C. got his mistress,—was't our friend,

His letter to the King, that did it all?
What paid the bloodless man for so much pains?
Our Lord the King has favourites manifold,
And shifts his ministry some once a month;   60
Our city gets new governors at whiles, —
But never word or sign, that I could hear,
Notified to this man about the streets
The King's approval of those letters conned
The last thing duly at the dead of night.
Did the man love his office? Frowned our Lord,
Exhorting when none heard — "Beseech me not!
"Too far above my people, — beneath me!
"I set the watch, — how should the people know?
"Forget them, keep me all the more in mind!"   70
Was some such understanding 'twixt the two?

    I found no truth in one report at least —
That if you tracked him to his home, down lanes
Beyond the Jewry, and as clean to pace,
You found he ate his supper in a room
Blazing with lights, four Titians on the wall,
And twenty naked girls to change his plate!
Poor man, he lived another kind of life
In that new stuccoed third house by the bridge,
Fresh-painted, rather smart than otherwise!   80
The whole street might o'erlook him as he sat,
Leg crossing leg, one foot on the dog's back,
Playing a decent cribbage with his maid
(Jacynth, you're sure her name was) o'er the cheese
And fruit, three red halves of starved winter-pears,
Or treat of radishes in April. Nine,
Ten, struck the church clock, straight to bed went he.

    My father, like the man of sense he was,
Would point him out to me a dozen times;
"'St — 'St," he'd whisper, "the Corregidor!"   90

I had been used to think that personage
Was one with lacquered breeches, lustrous belt,
And feathers like a forest in his hat,
Who blew a trumpet and proclaimed the news,
Announced the bull-fights, gave each church its turn,
And memorized the miracle in vogue!
He had a great observance from us boys;
We were in error; that was not the man.

   I'd like now, yet had haply been afraid,
To have just looked, when this man came to die,   100
And seen who lined the clean gay garret-sides
And stood about the neat low truckle-bed,
With the heavenly manner of relieving guard.
Here had been, mark, the general-in-chief,
Thro' a whole campaign of the world's life and death,
Doing the King's work all the dim day long,
In his old coat and up to knees in mud,
Smoked like a herring, dining on a crust, —
And, now the day was won, relieved at once!
No further show or need for that old coat,   110
You are sure, for one thing! Bless us, all the while
How sprucely we are dressed out, you and I!
A second, and the angels alter that.
Well, I could never write a verse, —could you?
Let's to the Prado and make the most of time.

DEVELOPMENT.

My Father was a scholar and knew Greek.
When I was five years old, I asked him once
"What do you read about?"

                         "The siege of Troy."

"What is a siege and what is Troy?"
                                    Whereat
He piled up chairs and tables for a town,
Set me a-top for Priam, called our cat
—Helen, enticed away from home (he said)
By wicked Paris, who couched somewhere close
Under the footstool, being cowardly,
But whom—since she was worth the pains, poor puss—   10
Towzer and Tray,—our dogs, the Atreidai,—sought
By taking Troy to get possession of
—Always when great Achilles ceased to sulk,
(My pony in the stable)—forth would prance
And put to flight Hector—our page-boy's self.
This taught me who was who and what was what:
So far I rightly understood the case
At five years old: a huge delight it proved
And still proves—thanks to that instructor sage
My Father, who knew better than turn straight   20
Learning's full flare on weak-eyed ignorance,
Or, worse yet, leave weak eyes to grow sand-blind,
Content with darkness and vacuity.

It happened, two or three years afterward,
That—I and playmates playing at Troy's Siege—
My Father came upon our make-believe.
"How would you like to read yourself the tale
Properly told, of which I gave you first
Merely such notion as a boy could bear?
Pope, now, would give you the precise account   30
Of what, some day, by dint of scholarship,
You'll hear—who knows?—from Homer's very mouth.
Learn Greek by all means, read the 'Blind Old Man,
Sweetest of Singers'—*tuphlos* which means 'blind,'
Hedistos which means 'sweetest.' Time enough!
Try, anyhow, to master him some day;

Until when, take what serves for substitute,
Read Pope, by all means!"
                              So I ran through Pope,
Enjoyed the tale—what history so true?
Also attacked my Primer, duly drudged,   40
Grew fitter thus for what was promised next—
The very thing itself, the actual words,
When I could turn—say, Buttmann to account.

Time passed, I ripened somewhat: one fine day,
"Quite ready for the Iliad, nothing less?
There's Heine, where the big books block the shelf:
Don't skip a word, thumb well the Lexicon!"

I thumbed well and skipped nowise till I learned
Who was who, what was what, from Homer's tongue,
And there an end of learning. Had you asked   50
The all-accomplished scholar, twelve years old,
"Who was it wrote the Iliad?"—what a laugh!
"Why, Homer, all the world knows: of his life
Doubtless some facts exist: it's everywhere:
We have not settled, though, his place of birth:
He begged, for certain, and was blind beside:
Seven cities claimed him—Scio, with best right,
Thinks Byron. What he wrote? Those Hymns we have.
Then there's the 'Battle of the Frogs and Mice,'
That's all—unless they dig 'Margites' up   60
(I'd like that) nothing more remains to know."

Thus did youth spend a comfortable time;
Until—"What's this the Germans say is fact
That Wolf found out first? It's unpleasant work
Their chop and change, unsettling one's belief:
All the same, while we live, we learn, that's sure."
So, I bent brow o'er *Prolegomena*.

And, after Wolf, a dozen of his like
Proved there was never any Troy at all,
Neither Besiegers nor Besieged, —nay, worse, —   70
No actual Homer, no authentic text,
No warrant for the fiction I, as fact,
Had treasured in my heart and soul so long—
Ay, mark you! and as fact held still, still hold,
Spite of new knowledge, in my heart of hearts
And soul of souls, fact's essence freed and fixed
From accidental fancy's guardian sheath.
Assuredly thenceforward—thank my stars!—
However it got there, deprive who could—
Wring from the shrine my precious tenantry,   80
Helen, Ulysses, Hector and his Spouse,
Achilles and his Friend?—though Wolf—ah, Wolf!
Why must he needs come doubting, spoil a dream?

But then "No dream's worth waking"—Browning says:
And here's the reason why I tell thus much.
I, now mature man, you anticipate,
May blame my Father justifiably
For letting me dream out my nonage thus,
And only by such slow and sure degrees
Permitting me to sift the grain from chaff,   90
Get truth and falsehood known and named as such.
Why did he ever let me dream at all,
Not bid me taste the story in its strength?
Suppose my childhood was scarce qualified
To rightly understand mythology,
Silence at least was in his power to keep:
I might have—somehow—correspondingly—
Well, who knows by what method, gained my gains,
Been taught, by forthrights not meanderings,
My aim should be to loathe, like Peleus' son,   100
A lie as Hell's Gate, love my wedded wife,

Like Hector, and so on with all the rest.
Could not I have excogitated this
Without believing such men really were?
That is—he might have put into my hand
The "Ethics"? In translation, if you please,
Exact, no pretty lying that improves,
To suit the modern taste: no more, no less—
The "Ethics": 't is a treatise I find hard
To read aright now that my hair is grey,   110
And I can manage the original.
At five years old—how ill had fared its leaves!
Now, growing double o'er the Stagirite,
At least I soil no page with bread and milk,
Nor crumple, dogsear and deface—boys' way.

MEMORABILIA.

I.

AH, did you once see Shelley plain,
    And did he stop and speak to you
And did you speak to him again?
    How strange it seems and new!

II.

But you were living before that,
    And also you are living after;
And the memory I started at—
    My starting moves your laughter.

Percy Bysshe Shelley

The Guardian-Angel

III.

I crossed a moor, with a name of its own
    And a certain use in the world no doubt,   10
Yet a hand's-breadth of it shines alone
    'Mid the blank miles round about:

IV.

For there I picked up on the heather
    And there I put inside my breast
A moulted feather, an eagle-feather!
    Well, I forget the rest.

THE GUARDIAN-ANGEL.

A PICTURE AT FANO.

I.

DEAR and great Angel, wouldst thou only leave
    That child, when thou hast done with him, for me!
Let me sit all the day here, that when eve
    Shall find performed thy special ministry,
And time come for departure, thou, suspending
Thy flight, mayst see another child for tending,
    Another still, to quiet and retrieve.

II.

Then I shall feel thee step one step, no more,
    From where thou standest now, to where I gaze,

—And suddenly my head is covered o'er   10
   With those wings, white above the child who prays
Now on that tomb—and I shall feel thee guarding
Me, out of all the world; for me, discarding
   Yon heaven thy home, that waits and opes its door.

III.

I would not look up thither past thy head
   Because the door opes, like that child, I know,
For I should have thy gracious face instead,
   Thou bird of God! And wilt thou bend me low
Like him, and lay, like his, my hands together,
And lift them up to pray, and gently tether   20
   Me, as thy lamb there, with thy garment's spread?

IV.

If this was ever granted, I would rest
   My head beneath thine, while thy healing hands
Close-covered both my eyes beside thy breast,
   Pressing the brain, which too much thought expands,
Back to its proper size again, and smoothing
Distortion down till every nerve had soothing,
   And all lay quiet, happy and suppressed.

V.

How soon all worldly wrong would be repaired!
   I think how I should view the earth and skies   30
And sea, when once again my brow was bared
   After thy healing, with such different eyes.
O world, as God has made it! All is beauty:
And knowing this, is love, and love is duty.
   What further may be sought for or declared?

VI.

Guercino drew this angel I saw teach
   (Alfred, dear friend!)—that little child to pray,
Holding the little hands up, each to each
   Pressed gently,—with his own head turned away
Over the earth where so much lay before him   40
Of work to do, though heaven was opening o'er him,
   And he was left at Fano by the beach.

VII.

We were at Fano, and three times we went
   To sit and see him in his chapel there,
And drink his beauty to our soul's content
   —My angel with me too: and since I care
For dear Guercino's fame (to which in power
And glory comes this picture for a dower,
   Fraught with a pathos so magnificent)—

VIII.

And since he did not work thus earnestly   50
   At all times, and has else endured some wrong—
I took one thought his picture struck from me,
   And spread it out, translating it to song.
My love is here. Where are you, dear old friend?
How rolls the Wairoa at your world's far end?
   This is Ancona, yonder is the sea.

BY THE FIRE-SIDE.

I.

How well I know what I mean to do
   When the long dark autumn-evenings come;
And where, my soul, is thy pleasant hue?
   With the music of all thy voices, dumb
In life's November too!

II.

I shall be found by the fire, suppose,
   O'er a great wise book as beseemeth age,
While the shutters flap as the cross-wind blows
   And I turn the page, and I turn the page,
Not verse now, only prose!   10

III.

Till the young ones whisper, finger on lip,
   "There he is at it, deep in Greek:
"Now then, or never, out we slip
   "To cut from the hazels by the creek
"A mainmast for our ship!"

IV

I shall be at it indeed, my friends:
   Greek puts already on either side
Such a branch-work forth as soon extends
   To a vista opening far and wide,
And I pass out where it ends.   20

V.

The outside-frame, like your hazel-trees:
  But the inside-archway widens fast,
And a rarer sort succeeds to these,
  And we slope to Italy at last
And youth, by green degrees.

VI.

I follow wherever I am led,
  Knowing so well the leader's hand:
Oh woman-country, wooed not wed,
  Loved all the more by earth's male-lands,
Laid to their hearts instead!   30

VII.

Look at the ruined chapel again
  Half-way up in the Alpine gorge!
Is that a tower, I point you plain,
  Or is it a mill, or an iron-forge
Breaks solitude in vain?

VIII.

A turn, and we stand in the heart of things;
  The woods are round us, heaped and dim;
From slab to slab how it slips and springs,
  The thread of water single and slim,
Through the ravage some torrent brings!   40

IX.

Does it feed the little lake below?
  That speck of white just on its marge

Is Pella; see, in the evening-glow,
   How sharp the silver spear-heads charge
When Alp meets heaven in snow!

X.

On our other side is the straight-up rock;
   And a path is kept 'twixt the gorge and it
By boulder-stones where lichens mock
   The marks on a moth, and small ferns fit
Their teeth to the polished block.   50

XI.

Oh the sense of the yellow mountain-flowers,
   And thorny balls, each three in one,
The chestnuts throw on our path in showers!
   For the drop of the woodland fruit's begun,
These early November hours,

XII.

That crimson the creeper's leaf across
   Like a splash of blood, intense, abrupt,
O'er a shield else gold from rim to boss,
   And lay it for show on the fairy-cupped
Elf-needled mat of moss,   60

XIII.

By the rose-flesh mushrooms, undivulged
   Last evening—nay, in to-day's first dew
Yon sudden coral nipple bulged,
   Where a freaked fawn-coloured flaky crew
Of toadstools peep indulged.

XIV.

And yonder, at foot of the fronting ridge
    That takes the turn to a range beyond,
Is the chapel reached by the one-arched bridge
    Where the water is stopped in a stagnant pond
Danced over by the midge.   70

XV.

The chapel and bridge are of stone alike,
    Blackish-grey and mostly wet;
Cut hemp-stalks steep in the narrow dyke.
    See here again, how the lichens fret
And the roots of the ivy strike!

XVI.

Poor little place, where its one priest comes
    On a festa-day, if he comes at all,
To the dozen folk from their scattered homes,
    Gathered within that precinct small
By the dozen ways one roams —   80

XVII.

To drop from the charcoal-burners' huts,
    Or climb from the hemp-dressers' low shed,
Leave the grange where the woodman stores his
        nuts,
    Or the wattled cote where the fowlers spread
Their gear on the rock's bare juts.

XVIII.

It has some pretension too, this front,
    With its bit of fresco half-moon-wise

Set over the porch, Art's early wont:
   'T is John in the Desert, I surmise,
But has borne the weather's brunt—   90

XIX.

Not from the fault of the builder, though,
   For a pent-house properly projects
Where three carved beams make a certain show,
   Dating—good thought of our architect's—
'Five, six, nine, he lets you know.

XX.

And all day long a bird sings there,
   And a stray sheep drinks at the pond at times;
The place is silent and aware;
   It has had its scenes, its joys and crimes,
But that is its own affair.   100

XXI.

My perfect wife, my Leonor,
   Oh heart, my own, oh eyes, mine too,
Whom else could I dare look backward for,
   With whom beside should I dare pursue
The path grey heads abhor?

XXII.

For it leads to a crag's sheer edge with them;
   Youth, flowery all the way, there stops—
Not they; age threatens and they contemn,
   Till they reach the gulf wherein youth drops,
One inch from life's safe hem!   110

The Refubbri Oratorio

Elizabeth Barrett Browning with Pen

XXIII.

With me, youth led . . . I will speak now,
  No longer watch you as you sit
Reading by fire-light, that great brow
  And the spirit-small hand propping it,
Mutely, my heart knows how —

XXIV.

When, if I think but deep enough,
  You are wont to answer, prompt as rhyme;
And you, too, find without rebuff
  Response your soul seeks many a time
Piercing its fine flesh-stuff.   120

XXV.

My own, confirm me! If I tread
  This path back, is it not in pride
To think how little I dreamed it led
  To an age so blest that, by its side,
Youth seems the waste instead?

XXVI.

My own, see where the years conduct!
  At first, 't was something our two souls
Should mix as mists do; each is sucked
  In each now: on, the new stream rolls,
Whatever rocks obstruct.   130

XXVII.

Think, when our one soul understands
  The great Word which makes all things new,

When earth breaks up and heaven expands,
   How will the change strike me and you
In the house not made with hands?

XXVIII.

Oh I must feel your brain prompt mine,
   Your heart anticipate my heart,
You must be just before, in fine,
   See and make me see, for your part,
New depths of the divine!   140

XXIX.

But who could have expected this
   When we two drew together first
Just for the obvious human bliss,
   To satisfy life's daily thirst
With a thing men seldom miss?

XXX.

Come back with me to the first of all,
   Let us lean and love it over again,
Let us now forget and now recall,
   Break the rosary in a pearly rain,
And gather what we let fall!   150

XXXI.

What did I say?—that a small bird sings
   All day long, save when a brown pair
Of hawks from the wood float with wide wings
   Strained to a bell: 'gainst noon-day glare
You count the streaks and rings.

XXXII.

But at afternoon or almost eve
  'T is better; then the silence grows
To that degree, you half believe
  It must get rid of what it knows,
Its bosom does so heave.   160

XXXIII.

Hither we walked then, side by side,
  Arm in arm and cheek to cheek,
And still I questioned or replied,
  While my heart, convulsed to really speak,
Lay choking in its pride.

XXXIV.

Silent the crumbling bridge we cross,
  And pity and praise the chapel sweet,
And care about the fresco's loss,
  And wish for our souls a like retreat,
And wonder at the moss.   170

XXXV.

Stoop and kneel on the settle under,
  Look through the window's grated square:
Nothing to see! For fear of plunder,
  The cross is down and the altar bare,
As if thieves don't fear thunder.

XXXVI.

We stoop and look in through the grate,
  See the little porch and rustic door,

Read duly the dead builder's date;
   Then cross the bridge that we crossed before,
Take the path again—but wait!   180

XXXVII.

Oh moment, one and infinite!
   The water slips o'er stock and stone;
The West is tender, hardly bright:
   How grey at once is the evening grown—
One star, its chrysolite!

XXXVIII.

We two stood there with never a third,
   But each by each, as each knew well:
The sights we saw and the sounds we heard,
   The lights and the shades made up a spell
Till the trouble grew and stirred.   190

XXXIX.

Oh, the little more, and how much it is!
   And the little less, and what worlds away!
How a sound shall quicken content to bliss,
   Or a breath suspend the blood's best play,
And life be a proof of this!

XL.

Had she willed it, still had stood the screen
   So slight, so sure, 'twixt my love and her:
I could fix her face with a guard between,
   And find her soul as when friends confer,
Friends—lovers that might have been.   200

XLI.

For my heart had a touch of the woodland-time,
    Wanting to sleep now over its best.
Shake the whole tree in the summer-prime,
    But bring to the last leaf no such test!
"Hold the last fast!" runs the rhyme.

XLII.

For a chance to make your little much,
    To gain a lover and lose a friend,
Venture the tree and a myriad such,
    When nothing you mar but the year can mend:
But a last leaf—fear to touch! 210

XLIII.

Yet should it unfasten itself and fall
    Eddying down till it find your face
At some slight wind—best chance of all!
    Be your heart henceforth its dwelling-place
You trembled to forestall!

XLIV.

Worth how well, those dark grey eyes,
    That hair so dark and dear, how worth
That a man should strive and agonize,
    And taste a veriest hell on earth
For the hope of such a prize! 220

XLV.

You might have turned and tried a man,
    Set him a space to weary and wear,

And prove which suited more your plan,
    His best of hope or his worst despair,
Yet end as he began.

XLVI.

But you spared me this, like the heart you are,
    And filled my empty heart at a word.
If two lives join, there is oft a scar,
    They are one and one, with a shadowy third;
One near one is too far.   230

XLVII.

A moment after, and hands unseen
    Were hanging the night around us fast;
But we knew that a bar was broken between
    Life and life: we were mixed at last
In spite of the mortal screen.

XLVIII.

The forests had done it; there they stood;
    We caught for a moment the powers at play:
They had mingled us so, for once and good,
    Their work was done—we might go or stay,
They relapsed to their ancient mood.   240

XLIX.

How the world is made for each of us!
    How all we perceive and know in it
Tends to some moment's product thus,
    When a soul declares itself—to wit,
By its fruit, the thing it does!

L.

Be hate that fruit or love that fruit,
  It forwards the general deed of man,
And each of the Many helps to recruit
  The life of the race by a general plan;
Each living his own, to boot.   250

LI.

I am named and known by that moment's feat;
  There took my station and degree;
So grew my own small life complete,
  As nature obtained her best of me—
One born to love you, sweet!

LII.

And to watch you sink by the fire-side now
  Back again, as you mutely sit
Musing by fire-light, that great brow
  And the spirit-small hand propping it,
Yonder, my heart knows how!   260

LIII.

So, earth has gained by one man the more,
  And the gain of earth must be heaven's gain
      too;
And the whole is well worth thinking o'er
  When autumn comes: which I mean to do
One day, as I said before.

PROSPICE.

FEAR death?—to feel the fog in my throat,
    The mist in my face,
When the snows begin, and the blasts denote
    I am nearing the place,
The power of the night, the press of the storm,
    The post of the foe;
Where he stands, the Arch Fear in a visible form,
    Yet the strong man must go:
For the journey is done and the summit attained,
    And the barriers fall,   10
Though a battle's to fight ere the guerdon be gained,
    The reward of it all.
I was ever a fighter, so—one fight more,
    The best and the last!
I would hate that death bandaged my eyes, and forbore,
    And bade me creep past.
No! let me taste the whole of it, fare like my peers
    The heroes of old,
Bear the brunt, in a minute pay glad life's arrears
    Of pain, darkness and cold.   20
For sudden the worst turns the best to the brave,
    The black minute's at end,
And the elements' rage, the fiend-voices that rave,
    Shall dwindle, shall blend,
Shall change, shall become first a peace out of pain,
    Then a light, then thy breast,
O thou soul of my soul! I shall clasp thee again,
    And with God be the rest!

Little Venice, London

Elizabeth Barrett Browning Aged 53

"O LYRIC LOVE."

O lyric Love, half angel and half bird
And all a wonder and a wild desire, —
Boldest of hearts that ever braved the sun,
Took sanctuary within the holier blue,
And sang a kindred soul out to his face, —
Yet human at the red-ripe of the heart—
When the first summons from the darkling earth
Reached thee amid thy chambers, blanched their blue,
And bared them of the glory—to drop down,
To toil for man, to suffer or to die, —   10
This is the same voice: can thy soul know change?
Hail then, and hearken from the realms of help!
Never may I commence my song, my due
To God who best taught song by gift of thee,
Except with bent head and beseeching hand—
That still, despite the distance and the dark,
What was, again may be; some interchange
Of grace, some splendour once thy very thought,
Some benediction anciently thy smile:
—Never conclude, but raising hand and head   20
Thither where eyes, that cannot reach, yet yearn
For all hope, all sustainment, all reward,
Their utmost up and on, —so blessing back
In those thy realms of help, that heaven thy home,
Some whiteness which, I judge, thy face makes proud,
Some wanness where, I think, thy foot may fall!

NEVER THE TIME AND THE PLACE.

NEVER the time and the place
   And the loved one all together!
This path—how soft to pace!
   This May—what magic weather!
Where is the loved one's face?
In a dream that loved one's face meets mine,
   But the house is narrow, the place is bleak
Where, outside, rain and wind combine
   With a furtive ear, if I strive to speak,
   With a hostile eye at my flushing cheek,   10
With a malice that marks each word, each sign!
O enemy sly and serpentine,
   Uncoil thee from the waking man!
      Do I hold the Past
      Thus firm and fast
   Yet doubt if the Future hold I can?
   This path so soft to pace shall lead
Thro' the magic of May to herself indeed!
Or narrow if needs the house must be,
Outside are the storms and strangers: we—   20
Oh, close, safe, warm sleep I and she,
   —I and she!

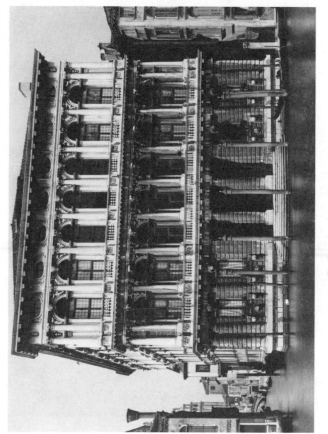

Ca Rezzonico, Venice

The Staircase of Ca Rezzonico, Venice

EPILOGUE to ASOLANDO.

At the midnight in the silence of the sleep-time,
   When you set your fancies free,
Will they pass to where—by death, fools think, im-
      prisoned—
Low he lies who once so loved you, whom you loved so,
      —Pity me?

Oh to love so, be so loved, yet so mistaken!
   What had I on earth to do
With the slothful, with the mawkish, the unmanly?
Like the aimless, helpless, hopeless, did I drivel
      —Being—who?   10

One who never turned his back but marched breast
      forward,
   Never doubted clouds would break,
Never dreamed, though right were worsted, wrong
      would triumph,
Held we fall to rise, are baffled to fight better,
      Sleep to wake.

No, at noonday in the bustle of man's work-time
   Greet the unseen with a cheer!
Bid him forward, breast and back as either should be,
"Strive and thrive!" cry "Speed,—fight on, fare ever
      There as here!"   20

EXPLANATORY NOTES

NARRATIVE POEMS

Incident of the French Camp
1842 *Dramatic Lyrics*
  The incident described in the poem took place at the storming of
Regensburg (Ratisbon) in Bavaria on the banks of the Danube on 23
April 1809 during Napoleon's Austrian campaign. Marshal Lannes,
who was killed a month later, fought particularly bravely, but the
story of the boy soldier is unrecorded in any history of the battle.
Browning claimed it was true, but that the soldier was a man—not a
boy.
  Line 29. *flag-bird* The Napoleonic eagle-emblem.
  29. *vans* Wings.

"How they brought the Good News from Ghent to Aix"
1845 *Dramatic Romances*
  The ride is an invented incident, which gives "a general impression
of the characteristic warfare and besieging which abounds in the annals
of Flanders." Browning wrote it at sea en route for Italy in 1844, which
may explain the hazy topography of the poem. The indirect route
taken by the three riders from Ghent in north-west Belgium to Aix-
la-Chapelle (Aachen) in Germany is 120 miles—considerably longer
than was prudent or necessary! Elizabeth Barrett admired the poem:
"you have the very trampling and breathing of the horses all through
... then the difficult management of the *three* horses, of the three
individualities; and Roland carrying the interest with him trium-
phantly." She particularly liked the sentiments of the last verse, "that
touch of natural feeling at the end, to prove that it was not in brutal
carelessness that the poor horse was driven through all that suffering."
The poem invites comparison with the sledge ride in "Ivàn Ivànovitch"
and also with "Childe Roland."

Line 10. *pique* Spur.

Halbert and Hob
1879 *Dramatic Idyls*
 Browning found the kernel of his story in Aristotle's *Ethics*, where anger and bad temper are shown to be natural to man. Aristotle recounts a story of four generations of a family ill-treating each other. Browning simplifies this and sets his story in the north of England at Christmas. That time of year helps him provide his conclusion that anger ultimately can only be tempered by supernatural means. The rough repetitious style is well-suited to the tale Browning tells.
 Line 24. *parish shell* Coffin provided by the local community rather than by the family.
 29. *mammoth* The secondary animal meaning supports the bestial imagery used throughout the poem.
 45. *Christmas* The sacred and supernatural legends concerning Christmastide can be seen in a host of poems from *Hamlet*, I, i, 157–164 to Hardy's "The Oxen."
 65. *Lear* Based on *King Lear*, III, vi, 81–82. The mad Lear utters the words "Is there any cause in nature that make these hard hearts?" after his mock-trial of the evil daughters Goneril and Regan.

The Pope and the Net
1889 *Asolando*
 This poem seems to have been Browning's invention. The speaker is a cardinal, more highly born than the man he has recently helped to elect Pope. The ironic detachment with which he tells his story acknowledges the superior cunning of the Pope whose simplicity and mock-humility have been a cover for his scheming and ambition. The verse-form (triplets in iambic septameter) helps to convey the speaker's tone of voice.
 Line 2. *Conclave* The assembly of cardinals which elects the Pope.
 9. *sword and keys* The insignia of the Pope. The sword refers to St. Peter's sword with which he cut off the high priest's servant's ear. The keys are the keys of Heaven.

Apparent Failure
1864 *Dramatis Personae*
 This deceptively simple story of an Englishman visiting the Paris morgue has its origin in Browning's own experiences in 1856 when he was living in Paris and attended the baptism of Napoleon III's son, the

Prince Imperial. To see the narrator as Browning would be quite wrong. He is, instead, a bluff, insular Englishman to whom the sight of the bodies of three suicides is profoundly disturbing. His attempts to come to terms with his experience display a personal inadequacy which is finally revealed in the platitudes of the final verse. The presence of the speaker gives a psychological complexity to what could have been a rather trivial narrative.

Line 7. *Congress* In 1856 the European powers met in Paris to end the Crimean War. Prince Gortschakoff was the Russian delegate. Cavour's appeal was for the recognition of an independent Piedmont, a move opposed by the Austrian Count von Buol-Schauenstein.

10. *Doric little Morgue* The public mortuary, built in the form of a Greek tomb during the First Republic, was situated near Notre-Dame on the Quai du Marché-Neuf. It was a common tourist sight. Charles Dickens described his visits there with a horrible fascination in *The Uncommercial Traveller*. The morgue was pulled down during the reconstruction of Paris in the 1860's. Browning's description of the interior is accurate, as can be seen from the contemporary illustration facing p. 13. Of 1745 suicides brought to the Paris morgue between 1826–46, 1414 died by drowning.

12. *Vaucluse* The Italian poet Petrarch lived for a time in Fontaine-de-Vaucluse, near Avignon. The fountain is the source of the river Sorgue.

39. *Tuileries* The Emperor's palace in Paris.

43. *Empire* The Second Empire, formed after Louis Bonaparte assumed the title Napoleon III in 1852.

46–47. *red ... black* The colour of the card suits—an allusion to gambling at *rouge et noir*. Verse 6 has been described by John Lucas as "one of the finest and most troubling pieces of verse Browning ever wrote."

Gold Hair: a Story of Pornic
1864 *Dramatis Personae*

Browning read this true story in Carou's *Histoire de Pornic*, which his father bought when they were on holiday together in Brittany near Pornic in 1862. The gold hoard was found in 1782 among the remains of Mlle Beaulon des Roussières. Browning uses the story to demonstrate human fallibility. The deliberately awkward narrative style emphasizes the obsessive avarice of the girl and lends an air of slight embarrassment to the bizarre tale. The conclusion is much more direct, and hits hard at contemporary Biblical scholarship. No questioning of the historical truth of the Bible, the speaker claims, can destroy our belief in original sin. The ambivalence in Browning's extended use of gold in the poem, as something pure and as something tarnished, can be paralleled in other poems, such as "Andrea del Sarto" and "Love among the Ruins."

Line. 16. *flix and floss* Down and fluffiness.

48. *death's privilege* Absolution.

86. *O cor . . .* Oh human heart, and blind affections.

90. *Louis-d'or* Gold coin, first issued in the reign of Louis XIII.

109. *humour* Disease (in the medieval sense of an excess of one of the four bodily humours, which in health determine a person's temperament).

128. *thirty pieces* Judas Iscariot was given thirty pieces of silver to betray Jesus. After he had hanged himself, the chief priests "took counsel, and bought with them the potter's field, to bury strangers in" (Matthew, 27:7).

143. *Essays-and-Reviews* The controversial *Essays and Reviews* (1860) were written by seven members of the Broad Church Party in opposition to the Tractarians. They proposed a scientific and historical interpretation of the scriptures, and initiated the Higher Criticism in England.

145. *Colenso* John William Colenso, first bishop of Natal, published *Critical Examination of the Pentateuch* in 1862, which questioned the historicity of the Bible.

149. *a lie* That Man is not corrupt.

The Statue and the Bust
1855 *Men and Women*
The poem's source is a Florentine legend, told to Browning by Seymour Kirkup, about the statue of Grand Duke Ferdinand di Medici in the Piazza SS. Annunziata seemingly looking towards a lady-love in the Riccardi Palace. Browning invented the bust of the lady, though there is a convenient niche under a window where one might have been placed. Details in the poem are inaccurate and anachronistic, because Browning was less concerned with historical accuracy than with the idea dominating the poem. This is to seize the moment, to make the most of a situation, rather than wither in inactivity—a

recurrent theme in Browning's work. By the end of the poem the nebulous Florentine narrator has disappeared, and Browning himself addresses the reader directly, one of the few occasions on which he does so.

Line 22. *encolure* Mane.

36. *crime* The absolute rule started by Cosimo di Medici in 1434 and continued by his son Piero, which suppressed Florentine liberty. Piero hardly deserves to be described as cursèd, as he wasn't a wicked man. Mairi Calcraft has suggested that cursèd means "afflicted by God" and refers to Piero's gout. Alternatively, Browning may be referring to Cosimo I (1519–74) whose son Francesco was notorious for his ineptitude and cruelty.

57. *catafalk* Funeral carriage.

72. *ave-bell* The bell calling people to prayer at dawn and evening.

94. *Arno bowers* The Duke invites the bride and groom to leave Florence and visit him in his villa at Petraja, in the country on the southern slopes of Mount Morello.

166. *Carver* A member of the famous della Robbia family—Luca, Andrea or Giovanni—all of whom had in fact died before the date of the commission. There is, however, a round bas-relief in enamelled terra-cotta of a young girl by Giovanni della Robbia in the Victoria and Albert Museum, London, which corresponds to the description in lines 188–195 and which may have given Browning the idea.

202. *John of Douay* Giambologna or Giovanni Bologna, born in Douai in 1529, accepted the commission from Ferdinand in 1601. The statue was not unveiled to the public until October 1608.

232. *pelf* Money.

233. *button goes* ... When any sort of counter does, it would be foolish to play with a rich coin.

237. *table's* ... When you play an improvised game using a hat for a board and when you play for a trifling stake.

242–243. The moral of the poem.

250. *De te, fabula* The story is about you.

Ivàn Ivànovitch
1879 *Dramatic Idyls*

Browning spent two months on a journey to Russia in 1834. That visit contributed effective local colour to "Ivàn Ivànovitch," but Browning probably read the story many years later, either in a French or English source. The poem is a study of guilt and justice. How guilty is Loùscha, and how just is Ivàn? The Russian narrator is in little doubt, as he guides the reader towards Ivàn's acquittal. But within the main narrative Loùscha's own stumbling story (followed by the speeches of the landowner and the priest) invites the reader's judgment. Tennyson was unconvinced of Loùscha's guilt and several modern critics have taken issue with Ivàn and the priest. A comparison of the ending of the poem with that in "The Statue and the Bust" would suggest that Browning is on Ivàn's side.

Line 14. *Peter's time* Peter the Great ruled Russia from 1682 to 1725 and opened the country to European influence.

19. *verst* A Russian measure, approximately .66 of a mile.

53. *Droug* Friend (pronounced Drook).

181. *Pope* Priest.

220. *green brass points* The third time this metaphor has been used, each time with an increased force. E. Warwick Slinn has noted how Browning makes the wolves slowly emerge, as from the depths of consciousness, gradually increasing their sensory impact.

282. *Stàrosta* Old man, village elder.

284. *Pomeschìk* Leading landowner.

317–19. *'Your young men shall see visions:'* Words from the prophet Joel, quoted by St. Peter at the beginning of his sermon on the day of Pentecost, during which he converted three thousand sceptics (Acts, 2:14–41).

324. *'Shall the dead praise thee?'* Psalm 88:10.

324–25. *'The whole live world . . .'* A biblical commonplace.

380–81. *Moses* Moses received the Commandments, written by God's hand on two tablets of stone, amid fire on Mount Sinai. (See Deuteronomy, 9:7–10:5.)

412. *Kremlin* Fortress, particularly that at Moscow.

421. *Kolokol* The large bell of the Kremlin.

Pan and Luna
1880 *Dramatic Idyls, Second Series*

This mysterious and elusive poem has its origin in three lines from Virgil's third Georgic: "'T was with gift of such snowy wool, if we may trust the tale, that Pan, Arcadia's God, charmed and beguiled thee, O Moon, calling thee to the depths of the woods; nor didst thou scorn his call." To Virgil the legend was an attempt by primitive man to explain the first eclipse of the moon; to Browning the story evoked the contradictory nature of human love. The narrator's position, as so often in Browning, helps the reader to respond to the poem. He starts confidently and objectively, but gets caught up in the sensuousness of the story he is telling, and finally is defeated by the ramifications of the narrative. The poem's subject may be said to be the reluctance of man to accept the blend of the physical and spiritual in human love; but such an explanation fails to capture the subtlety and the magic of a most unusual poem.

    Epigraph If it is worthy of belief.

    Line 28. *uncinct* Uncircled.

    34. *succourable* Helpful.

    45. *sister paps* Breasts.

    46. *consummate circle* The narrator stops himself from going into more intimate physical detail. Instead, he uses the word "circle" in two ways. It is an image of infinity as well as of female sexuality. The narrator, therefore, suggests an infinite spiritual beauty allied to the finite and earthly.

    58. *conceits* Fancies.

    59. *Amphitrite's dome* The sea.

    71. *learned Virgil* In the third Georgic, Virgil advises shepherds to destroy rams with black tongues lest this should taint the white fleece of their offspring. It is while giving this practical advice about white wool that, as a three-line aside, he mentions Pan's seduction of Luna.

    84. *sward* Skin.

LOVE POEMS

Song
1845 *Dramatic Romances*
    This lyric, almost stuttering with excitement, communicates the speaker's feelings by his very inability to articulate them. The poem has little autobiographical significance in spite of its date; it was not written specifically for Elizabeth Barrett, although she admired it when she read it in proof. Characteristic of Browning is the gold metaphor and the rich sensuousness of the woman's hair. Both recur frequently in Browning's poetry, and are joined together in a number of poems including "Gold Hair" and "Porphyria's Lover."

Ask not one least word of praise
1884 *Ferishtah's Fancies*
    A companion-piece to the previous poem—but in a minor key. Written forty years later, when Browning's affections were engaged

by Katharine Bronson, the delicate language conveys a sense of questioning wonder.

Meeting at Night
Parting at Morning
1845 *Dramatic Romances*

These linked poems contrast the questing lover's excited anticipation before meeting his girl-friend with his firm acceptance of his place in the world the following morning. "Meeting at Night" is a series of sense-impressions in a familiar landscape muffled in darkness; "Parting at Morning" is a confident statement in a sun-drenched open scene where the eye explores the far horizon. When questioned about the meaning of the last line of "Parting at Morning," Browning replied, "It is *his* confession of how fleeting is the belief (implied in the first part) that such raptures are self-sufficient and enduring—as for the time they appear."

Now
1889 *Asolando*

This poem celebrates the ecstasy of sexual passion and man's desire to sublimate it into something more lasting. For all the speaker's confidence, one is reminded of Browning's comments on the previous poem. His statement (quoted above) about the lover falsely believing his raptures to be self-sufficient and enduring was written in 1889, the year of "Now."

Love among the Ruins
1855 *Men and Women*

The manuscript of "Love among the Ruins" is entitled "Sicilian Pastoral." Although attempts have been made to locate the scene in Sicily, just outside Syracuse, the setting is more likely an amalgam of the Roman Campagna, which Browning frequently visited, and the ruins of Nineveh, Babylon and the Egyptian Thebes. New excavations had been made on all three sites in the decade before the poem was written. Thoughts of this romantic past intrude on the mind of Browning's young shepherd as he makes his way across the grassy plain towards his waiting girl-friend. He contrasts the unfocussed, dull modern scene with the vital and powerful past, which he also sees in strong sexual terms. His attempt to reconcile the limited, attainable present with the assertive, attractive but unattainable past, provides the conflict and psychological interest of the poem.

Line 41. *houseleek* A pink-flowered plant found on old walls and roofs.

65. *causeys* Causeways.

Two in the Campagna
1855 Men and Women

The Campagna is the grassy plain outside Rome dotted with the ruins of ancient tombs and broken aqueducts. During the nineteenth century it was a popular place for picnics and walks. The Brownings frequently visited it during 1854 with the actress Fanny Kemble and her sister Mrs. Sartoris. The lover in the poem uses details of the scene in an attempt to express his feelings of frustration.

Line 8. *thread* One of the features of the Campagna is the gossamer carpet spun every morning by millions of tiny spiders, which is unnoticed until caught by the sun.

14. *ruin* The spirit of the dead past pervades the poem.

17. *beetles* This microscopic detail of the blind beetles groping among the honey reflects the lovers' inability to come to terms with their infinite passion.

48. *rose* Cf. *Othello*, v, 2, 13–15: "When I have plucked the rose / I cannot give it vital growth again, / It needs must wither."

55. *Fixed* Guided. There may also be an allusion to Shakespeare's Sonnet 116 in which love is described as "an ever fixed mark ... a star to every wand'ring bark."

In the Doorway
1864 Dramatis Personae

This is part of a linked sequence of poems, *James Lee's Wife*, set in Sainte Marie, near Pornic, in Brittany, where Browning was staying when he wrote them in 1863. They tell the story of a breaking marriage—"people newly-married, trying to realize a dream of being sufficient to each other, in a foreign land ... and finding it break up,—the man being *tired* first." The sequence has some similarities with George Meredith's *Modern Love* (1862), although, unlike Meredith, it has no autobiographical relevance. In "In the Doorway" the wife equates the approach of winter and the bleak autumnal countryside outside her cottage with the emotional coldness of her marriage. At the end she still has enough spirit to challenge the seemingly inevitable.

Line 4. *leeward* Side sheltered from the wind.

6. *"Good fortune ..."* An old country saying relating to the yearly emigration of the swallows.

19. *bent* Stalk of coarse beach grass.

23. *spirit* Man's God-given potential.

27–28. *Oh, live* ... There is a sense of desperate hope in these lines. James Lee's wife refuses to succumb to the universal cold.

A Woman's Last Word
1855 *Men and Women*

The intimacy of this poem is emphasized by the verse form with its short lines and close rhyme. The woman's words are spoken—or whispered—into the ear of her husband as the couple lie in bed. After a quarrel she pretends to make a surrender of herself, body and soul, to him. In fact her last word gives her the ascendancy over him.

Line 9. *creature* The evil which has caused the quarrel, here personified as an animal or Satan.

14. *False to thee* Since it seems false to thee.

26. *as I ought* In my role as a submissive wife. In fact the poem questions the Victorian assumption of male domination in marriage.

The Lost Mistress
1845 *Dramatic Romances*

This poem sees truth as relative in the context of time. The truth is that the woman has called an end to an affair, but her lover, in accepting the present situation, hopes that time may heal the rift. His apparently inconsequential remarks refer frequently to change and the passing of time.

Confessions
1864 *Dramatis Personae*

Augustine Birrell praised "Confessions" as long ago as 1884. Describing the poem as "veritable Browning," he stated it was "one of those poetical audacities none ever dared but the Danton of modern poetry. Audacious in its familiar realism, in its total disregard of poetical environment, in its rugged abruptness: but supremely successful, and alive with emotion." The poem's humour and easy conversational style have a similar appeal today. The illicit love affair—and the reader's tacit approval—contrast strongly with the unfulfilled relationship in "The Statue and the Bust."

Inapprehensiveness
1889 *Asolando*

The genesis of this poem occurred in the late summer of 1889 when Browning was staying in Asolo. The elderly speaker and his younger companion are modelled on Browning himself and the attractive middle-aged American, Katharine Bronson. The poem reflects the frustration Browning was experiencing in his failure to communicate his feelings towards Mrs. Bronson. Like the speaker in the poem, Browning chose to keep their relationship on a superficial literary-aesthetic level, rather than endanger it with a declaration of love which might be rebuffed. The suppressed passion of the speaker's thoughts is well conveyed by the disjointed syntax.

Line 10. *perspective glass* Telescope.

12. *Ruskin* John Ruskin, the art critic, whose *Stones of Venice* dealt with the region around Asolo.

16. *distent* Stretched.

19. *wilding* Literally, a wild plant; figuratively, a spontaneous, impulsive thought.

22. *sward* Turf.

32. *Vernon Lee* Pseudonym of Violet Paget, a young English writer just establishing a reputation. She opposed Ruskin's views on the morality of art.

A Serenade at the Villa
1855 *Men and Women*

The title belies the poem. No serenade is audible. No lady is visible. Instead there is a heavy atmosphere, darkness and silence. Time seems to be standing still; the reader is surprised when the east turns grey to signal another day. The triple enclosure (shuttered villa, garden with its iron gate, and tent of heaven) weighs heavily and contributes to the poem's lack of life and feeling of pain. In this ambience the serenader has no chance. He rehearses two possible responses to his song—one positive, one negative—but already knows that the invisible, enclosed lady will cruelly reject him. The serenader's extraordinary use of grotesque imagery gives an atmosphere of suffocating despair to his predicament. One is left asking whether the situation is as bad as he claims, or whether the description of the night's events is the product of his diseased love-crazed imagination.

Line 6. *fly* Firefly.

7. *worm* Glow-worm.

9. *forbore a term* Were quiet for a moment.

12. *suspired for proof* Sighed to show she was in pain.

25. *passed away* Literally, left; metaphorically, despaired and died.

39. *taskmaster* God.

53. *die in peace* She is not physically dying, but she sees life as a living death.

DRAMATIC MONOLOGUES

My Last Duchess
1842 *Dramatic Lyrics*
This perfect dramatic monologue has almost no historical basis. The most convincing hypothesis relates the Duke to Alfonso II of Ferrara (1533–1597) and the Duchess to his first wife Lucrezia di Medici, who died aged 17 in 1561. This identification is unlikely to have been in Browning's mind when he wrote the poem, because on its first publication the setting was loosely described as Italy rather than Ferrara. It is, therefore, best to see the poem as a wholly imaginative exploration of Renaissance values and warped psychology. The Duchess's fresh spontaneity is contrasted with the Duke's obsessiveness. There is an unnerving mixture of cruelty and refinement in his character; his audacious treatment of his late wife, his veiled threats, are presented in such a reasonable way that the reader is momentarily convinced by his speech. Technically the poem is remarkable. In particular, Browning's skilful use of rhyme in the couplets contributes to the silky urbanity of the Duke's words.
Line 3. *Frà Pandolf* An imaginary monk-painter.
25. *favour* A jewel or brooch.
45. *I gave commands* i.e. to murder her.
56. *Claus of Innsbruck* An imaginary sculptor.

Porphyria's Lover
1836 *Monthly Repository*
Like "My Last Duchess" this poem is about sexual possessiveness. The speaker, a young forester on a large estate, has fallen in love with Porphyria, the lady from the manor-house. When she visits his cottage on the evening of a ball, he murders her in a lunatic attempt to preserve their relationship. This early poem, therefore, displays Browning's interest in morbid psychology. The details of the setting are extremely well delineated, as the speaker tells his story to someone searching the grounds for the missing lady. His mad logic is horribly convincing: cocooned in his own world, he pays no obvious attention to the person he is addressing.

Line 24. *vainer ties* Porphyria's friendship with her upper-class companions, of whom he is jealous.

Soliloquy of the Spanish Cloister
1842 *Dramatic Lyrics*

This poem should not be taken too seriously. Jealousy is shown to have its melodramatic and humorous side. Browning zestfully portrays the exaggerated maliciousness of the monk-speaker when confronted with the serene goodness of his equally insufferable gardener brother. The pettiness of institutional life, as well as the sexual frustration of someone not intended for celibacy, are celebrated in this comic tour-de-force.

Line 10. *Salve tibi* "How are you?" The rule was to speak only Latin during mealtimes in this monastery.

14. *oak-galls* Growths or excrescences on oak-leaves caused by a gall-fly. They would be used for making ink for the monastery.

16. *Swine's Snout* Dandelion (*rostrum porcinum* in Latin). The speaker's patience is snapping, as he remembers the fussy conversation of Brother Lawrence.

22. *chaps* Mouth.

31. *Barbary corsair* Pillaging pirate on the north coast of Africa. The appellation is absurd. The speaker's description of the girls reflects his own interest in them—not Brother Lawrence's.

36. *As I do* The speaker obeys the outward forms of the Christian life, which Brother Lawrence neglects. The inner belief eludes him.

39. *Arian* The Arians were heretics who denied the Trinity.

49. *Galatians* Browning errs. The passage in question is Deuteronomy, 28:16–44.

56. *Manichee* Another type of heretic who believed that Satan was co-eternal with God.

60. *Belial* One of the followers of Satan.

62. *woeful sixteenth print* A particularly pornographic picture in the lewd French book he possesses.

70. *Hy, Zy, Hine* Probably a mocking of the chapel bell which has just started to ring.

71. *Plena gratiâ ...* A dismissive "Hail Mary!"

A Toccata of Galuppi's
1855 *Men and Women*

This virtuoso musical poem, which deals with the transitoriness of life, is as light and insubstantial as the melody of one of Galuppi's toccatas. Browning captures the sound of the clavichord in the varied metre with its basic anapaestic beat. The poem is also dazzling in its original use of the dramatic monologue form. A Victorian scientist addresses the spirit of Baldassare Galuppi, the eighteenth-century Venetian composer, who speaks back to him through the music, creating a scene during the Carnival a hundred years earlier. The contrast between the Venetian social butterflies and the useful scientist brings out that conflict between moral judgment and personal sympathy so characteristic of Browning's dramatic monologues. The portrayal of the narrator deserves particular attention.

Line 6. *Saint Mark's* The cathedral of Venice. The Doge was the ruler of the city. Every year he used to drop a ring into the Adriatic from the side of his ceremonial state barge to symbolize a wedding with the sea, indicative of the maritime power of Venice.

8. *Shylock's bridge* The Rialto.

18. *Toccatas* Fast-moving key-pieces, intended to demonstrate dexterity of touch.

19. *lesser thirds* This and later musical terms illustrate and reinforce the lovers' feelings. The music reflects their moods.

The Bishop orders his Tomb at Saint Praxed's Church
1845 *Hood's Magazine*

John Ruskin felt that this poem epitomized the Renaissance spirit. He isolated its "worldliness, inconsistency, pride, hypocrisy, ignorance of itself, love of art, luxury, and of good Latin." He might have added its callousness, because it is the Bishop's callous, silent, illegitimate sons, clustered round his bed who chill the air and give his speech a despairing poignancy. He knows that they will cheat him, as he has cheated his predecessor Gandolf, and fail to give him the tomb he covets. Try as hard as he may, he knows he cannot bribe them with things they will automatically take when he is dead. Nor can he bribe God. What survives at the end of the poem is a worldly man left only with the sensuous enjoyment of dying. That he is a thief, lecher, liar, a man totally unsuited to his religious calling, matters little. We watch his end with a similar awe to that experienced in watching the death of Faust. The dislocations and slight haziness of the language suggest a dying man, but it is the verbal richness of the voluptuary which remains permanently in the memory.

Line 1. *Vanity* ... The bishop chooses a text from Ecclesiastes, 1:2 as a prelude to his speech, which shows his moral awareness of his sinful life.

14. *Saint Praxed* Browning visited the church of Santa Prassede in Rome in 1844, which gave him the idea for the poem.

25. *basalt* Black stone.

26. *tabernacle* Stone canopy over his tomb.

31. *onion-stone* Cheap marble.

34. *conflagration* It seems the bishop set fire to part of his church so that in the confusion he could steal a lump of lapis lazuli, a semi-precious blue stone.

41. *olive-frail* Basket for gathering olives.

49. *Jesu church* Chiesa del Gesù in Rome.

51. *Swift as a weaver's* ... Another Biblical quotation, this time from Job, 7:6.

58. *tripod, thyrsus* Two pagan details. A tripod was a bronze, three-legged stool associated with the priestesses at Delphi; a thyrsus was an ornamental staff carried by followers of Bacchus.

66. *travertine* A cheap, soft, light-coloured, calcareous rock found near Rome.

77. *Tully* Cicero, whose writing is renowned for its classical purity.

79. *Ulpian* Ulpianus, a later Roman writer, inferior to Cicero.

90. *sculptor's-work* He visualizes his physical self being transmuted into a stone effigy.

95. *at his sermon* St. Praxed was a female saint. The bishop is becoming confused as death approaches, and mistakes her for Jesus.

99. *elucescebat* "He was illustrious." The bishop is laughing at the bad Latin he has had inscribed from Ulpian on his rival's tomb.

108. *Term* Pedestal-bust.

116. *Gritstone* Sandstone.

Fra Lippo Lippi
1855 Men and Women
The idea for this exuberant poem came from Browning's reading of Vasari's "Life of Fra Filippo Lippi" and from seeing Lippo's painting of *The Coronation of the Virgin* in the Galleria dell'Accademia, Florence, in the early 1850's. The story of the monk Lippo escaping from Cosimo di Medici's palace to pursue a group of girls is from Vasari, but his capture by the watch is Browning's own invention—as is Lippo's promise to "make amends" by painting the *Coronation* for the nuns of St. Ambrogio's convent. Browning uses the monologue to put forward Lippo's artistic creed, which, with its emphasis on realism and service to God, is similar to Browning's own. Lippo is an artist in words. His language is fecund, fresh and imaginative.

Images tumble from his lips in quick succession to create a series of imaginative pictures. The poem is full of movement. The reactions of Lippo's captor-listeners are created as vividly as are the episodes from Lippo's past life. After such a torrent of words – abuse, reminiscence, cajoling, and impudent bribery—it is not surprising Lippo is allowed to go free at the end of the poem.

Line 3. *Zooks* "Gadzooks!"—a mild oath deriving from the nails or "hooks" used in the crucifixion of Jesus.

7. *Carmine's my cloister* I should be safe inside my monastery in Santa Maria Carmine.

17. *Cosimo* Cosimo the Elder (1389–1464), ruler of Florence and patron of the arts.

21. *you, sir* Captain of the watch.

25. *Judas* Lippo flatters the watch by suggesting that some of them might serve as models for his paintings, and also insults them by suggesting that they would be used to represent evil or ignoble people.

53ff. *Flower o' the broom* Here and later in the poem, Lippo sings fragments of lyrical Tuscan folk-songs called *stornelli*.

121. *Eight* The Florentine magistrates.

130. *antiphonary* Book of choral music.

139. *Camaldolese* An independent order of Benedictines who had a monastery near Florence. The Preaching Friars were the Dominicans whose chief Florentine painter was Fra Angelico.

146. *folk at church* Notice the way in which Lippo creates this vivid picture in 18 lines of spontaneous verse. One idea engenders the next. They follow each other so fast he can hardly get the words out.

148. *cribs* Petty thefts.

172. *funked* Extinguished itself in smoke.

189. *Giotto* The early painter and innovator, whose work does not possess the realism of Lippo's.

227. *Corner-house* The Medici-Riccardi palace. See line 18.

235. *Brother Angelico* Fra Angelico, who with Lorenzo Monaco (Brother Lorenzo) represents an earlier style of painting.

276. *Guidi* Tommaso Guidi—known as Masaccio—painter of the frescoes in the Brancacci chapel in the Carmine. Browning thought him younger than Lippo, and to be Lippo's pupil. The reverse is true.

313. *no blot . . . Nor blank* The world we live in is neither a negative nor a bland place.

328. *toasted side* St. Laurence was martyred by being roasted to death on a grid-iron. The destruction of the faces of his torturers in the fresco shows the superstition of the people.

346. *Sant' Ambrogio's* A convent in Florence for which Lippo painted his *Coronation of the Virgin* (see p. 91). The description of this painting in the rest of the poem follows the general design of Lippo's work and is mostly accurate. The figure in the bottom right-hand corner, thought by Browning to be Lippo, is in fact Canon Francesco Maringhi who commissioned the painting.

347. *cast o' my office* Example of my work.

351. *orris-root* Root of iris used for perfume.

358. *Uz* Job's home.

377. *Iste perfecit opus* Similar words appear on a scroll near the figure Browning thought to be Lippo in the painting. "He created the work."

380. *kirtles* Skirts.

381. *hot cockles* A country game. In this context it suggests sexual dalliance.

387. *Saint Lucy* Lippo has ironically portrayed the wanton niece of the prior as the virginal Saint Lucy.

Andrea del Sarto
1855 *Men and Women*
    Browning is reputed to have sent this poem to his friend John Kenyon who had asked him for a copy of the self-portrait of Andrea del Sarto sitting beside his wife, which hung in the Pitti Palace in Florence. Browning went to Vasari for details of Andrea's life, and from him obtained the poem's sub-title "The Faultless Painter." Vasari saw in Andrea's work evidence of "a certain timidity of mind, a sort of diffidence and want of force," which meant that his paintings lacked grandeur and inspiration, although they were technically brilliant. Browning equates Andrea's artistic failing with those of his personal life. He is totally devoted to his faithless wife Lucrezia; aware of her infidelities, he allows her to dominate his life. In the poem Lucrezia listens coldly, waiting for an assignation with her lover, while Andrea talks haltingly about the failure of his past life and his artistic hopes. He knows that he is second-rate, half-blames Lucrezia for his lack of success, but finally admits his own responsibility. The blank verse is enervated, the thought lacks direction, and the sentences are syntactically complex and disjointed. All contribute to the ignobility and pathos of Andrea himself.

    Line 5. *friend's friend* The friend of her lover, the "cousin."

    15. *Fiesole* Hill-town outside Florence.

57. *cartoon* Full size design on paper for a painting.

65. *Legate* Representative of the Pope.

76. *Someone* Michelangelo.

93. *Morello* Mountain in the Apennines north of Florence.

97. *man's reach* ... An expression of the "philosophy of the imper-
fect," an idea common to Browning's thought.

105. *Urbinate* Raphael—who came from Urbino.

106. *George Vasari* Pupil of Andrea's and author of *Lives of the
Artists* from where Browning obtained details for the poem.

130. *Agnolo* Michelangelo.

146. *Paris lords* In 1518 Andrea had been invited to Paris as a court-
painter for Francis I of France. Lucrezia lured him back to Italy when
she became bored, and persuaded him to misappropriate money Fran-
cis had lent Andrea. Andrea, therefore, feels guilty whenever he sees
Frenchmen in Florence.

210. *cue-owls* Small owls. Browning anglicizes their name from the
Italian *ciù*.

250. *father and my mother* Vasari accused Andrea of abandoning his
parents for Lucrezia's family.

263. *Leonard* Leonardo da Vinci.

A Grammarian's Funeral
1855 *Men and Women*
   Walter Bagehot described Browning as a poet of the grotesque. No
poem better fulfils this description than "A Grammarian's Funeral."
Almost every feature—its plot, its chief character, its irregular
rhythms, its strained diction and syntax—is grotesque. The poem
follows the funeral procession of an early Renaissance scholar, whose
corpse is borne on the shoulders of his former pupils, one of whom
speaks to and encourages the others as they make their way up a
mountain-side. In the world's eyes the scholar is a dry pedant, but to
his followers he is a hero worthy of burial on the summit of the
mountain. The grammarian has fulfilled Andrea del Sarto's aspira-
tions: his reach has exceeded his grasp. He has almost succeeded in his
mighty task to know and understand all his field of human knowledge.
By his efforts he has made the Renaissance possible. Browning un-
doubtedly admires the grammarian's philosophy of life. Sadly it is
unfashionable today to take this poem seriously. Much contemporary
criticism interprets the poem satirically. While there may be some
intentional irony in the portrayal of the students, the object of their

enthusiasm is praiseworthy. The poem is intended as a challenge to the readers' latent conservatism.

Line 3. *crofts* Small-holdings.

3. *thorpes* Villages. The landscape is portrayed symbolically. The journey from the plain to the mountain-top symbolizes different stages in the grammarian's life.

12. *Chafes in the censer* Frets to be free.

22. *warning* Signal for the procession to start.

34. *Apollo* The grammarian was born with the gifts of the Greek god of poetry. i.e. he was a creative artist when young.

47. *scroll* Manuscripts—probably Greek manuscripts from Constantinople.

50. *gowned him* Became a scholar.

86. *Calculus* Gall-stones.

88. *Tussis* A cough.

95. *hydroptic* Excessive thirsting for knowledge.

120. *Misses an unit* Misses by only one unit.

129–131. *Hoti ... oun ... de* Greek particles—that, then and towards.

134. *purlieus* Haunts.

"*Imperante Augusto Natus Est—*"
1889 *Asolando*

Browning chooses pagan Rome just before the birth of Christ as the setting for this poem. A self-important Roman senator confides in his friend Publius certain worries as they wait their turn in the public baths. He shows scepticism at the deification of Augustus, a scepticism which leads to the central concern of the poem: human pride and fear of retribution. In an attempt to ward off the gods' anger, all-powerful Augustus abases himself as a beggar one day a year. The confused morality of the pagan world is contrasted with implied Christian values, imminent, but as yet unknown to the speaker. In the poem Browning expresses the unease caused by the spiritual emptiness of a rich secular society.

Title "He was born in the reign of Augustus." This prophecy of the birth of Christ is taken from the Christian *Sibylline Oracles* (see lines 158–159) which purport to be the words of the Erythraean sibyl.

Line 8. *Lucius Varius Rufus* Minor Augustan poet. He composed a panegyric to Augustus which is now lost.

11. *Flaccus* Horace—who was short and stout. An anachronism because Horace, like Varius, was dead by 2 B.C.

12. *Epos* Epic.

16. *Mæcenas* Virgil's patron and friend of Augustus. Horace refers to his aristocratic birth. The Roman literary circle is shown to be smug and complacent.

17. *quadrans* Small coin.

17. *Thermæ* Baths. Here a meeting-place.

34. *free hand* This long list of Augustus's achievements, his gifts to Rome and her Empire, come from Suetonius, who said that Augustus "could justly boast that he had found Rome built of brick and left it in marble."

73. *less famed* The limitations of the speaker are shown in this line.

94. *Fulgurant* Flashing like lightning.

101. *fane* Temple.

104. *Suburra* A disreputable district in Rome.

109. *quæstor* ... Four municipal officers, in ascending order of importance.

109. *Pol* An oath, "By Pollux!"

113. *quarter-as* Coin of little value.

140. *whoso conquers* In a Roman triumph, the victor rode in his chariot to the temple of Jupiter on the Capitoline hill. A slave held the ceremonial gold crown above his head, while a scourge and other implements were attached to his chariot to mollify the jealousy of the gods. The reference to a crucifixion in line 151 anticipates the introduction of the birth of Jesus at the end of the poem.

155. *predecessor* Uranus, chief of the Titans, overthrown by his son Saturn, who in turn was overthrown by Jupiter.

163. *strigils* Scrapers used in the baths.

Up at a Villa—Down in the City
1855 *Men and Women*
The fun starts with the see-saw title and the garrulous narrator, an "Italian person of quality" who speaks the poem either to himself or to some anonymous listener. The affected voice of the impoverished gentleman extolling the excitement of the city over the boredom of the country is so preposterous that he can't be taken seriously. He doesn't "distinguish," but merely enthuses and exaggerates. Subjective statements take the place of argument. The speaker's emotional response is extremely immature; he takes a child's delight in cheap excitement and pageantry, observing life rather than participating in it. The language he uses is equally superficial and comic. He can't articulate clearly and he lacks the poetic imagination to use metaphor successfully.

Browning expects his readers to bring their judgment to the incongruous town and country scenes. We leave the speaker's window-seat and taste the freedom of the country as well as the repression of the town. But we do not automatically opt for the country. We feel the need of the excitement, the spiritual and intellectual challenge of the city to balance rustic tranquillity and hard work. Man needs *both*. He also needs to work for his money, unlike the person of quality who is content to observe and complain about his poverty. Perhaps if he worked in either city or villa, he would grow up?

Line 9. *shag* Tangled mass.

12. *white as a curd* An unattractive simile. Notice how the speaker mixes country and town. One would associate curd with the country.

39. *diligence* Stage-coach.

42. *Pulcinello-trumpet* A showman's trumpet announcing the performance of a puppet-show.

52. *seven swords* Symbolizing the seven sorrows of Mary. Religion for the speaker is this gaudy doll-image of the Virgin Mary rather than serious Lent lectures.

60. *penitents* In the Lenten procession. Their dramatic costume and hooded faces would appeal to the speaker.

62. *Duke's guard* Probably Grand Duke Leopold II of Tuscany, who was particularly oppressive. (See line 46.)

"Childe Roland to the Dark Tower came"
1855 *Men and Women*

Browning claimed that *Childe Roland* came upon him "as a kind of dream." He had to write it then and there, and finished it in one day. He resisted all attempts by his friends and contemporaries to find a conscious allegory in the poem. Like T.S. Eliot's *The Waste Land*, "Childe Roland" reveals both a conscious and a subconscious use of its author's reading. Debts to Arthurian romance, to Shakespeare, Bunyan, Donne, Dante, to fairy-tale and to folk-lore are all evident. Yet the poem is greater than the sum of its parts. The landscape Roland travels through is indeed a waste-land, although his imagination makes it seem worse than it really is. The mental stress he undergoes is greater than his physical hardship. He almost succumbs to despair before he comes across the tower and blows his horn. Pressed to explain the meaning of the poem, Browning agreed that it could just about be summarized by the phrase "he that endureth to the end shall be saved." In fact, "Childe Roland" is much more than this. Although set in the form of a dramatic monologue, it is, as Ian Jack has shown, a personal poem, unconsciously inspired by Browning's own deepest fears of failure and spiritual inadequacy.

Epigraph From *King Lear* (III, 4, 187) during the storm on the heath when Edgar, disguised as poor mad Tom, jabbers to Lear whose wits are beginning to turn. If nothing else, this introduces the atmosphere of mental stress, so important to the poem. *Childe* is a young aspirant to knighthood.

Line 48. *estray* Stray animal.

58. *cockle, spurge* Weeds.

66. *Calcine* Burn to powder.

68. *bents* Very coarse grasses.

76. *stiff blind horse* Browning claimed that the horse figured on a tapestry he owned. (See photograph facing p. 128.)

80. *colloped* Lacerated.

133. *cirque* Circular depression like a natural amphitheatre.

135. *mews* Prison.

143. *Tophet* An Hebraic name for Hell.

153. *boils* Notice the anthropomorphic use of nature. Roland invests the landscape with the pain from his own mental suffering.

160. *Apollyon* The devil (from Revelation) or a winged monster in *The Pilgrim's Progress*.

161. *dragon-penned* With feathers like a dragon.

182. *fool's heart* See Psalms, 14:1. "The Lord hath said in his heart, There is no God."

203. *slug-horn* Originally the word meant "war-cry" or "slogan." Here it means horn used to blow a challenge—with an inevitable reminiscence of Roland's horn and his defeat at Roncesvalles.

PERSONAL POEMS

House

1876 *Pacchiarotto*

The strength of feeling in this poem is surprising. The speaker-poet's ironic mockery suggests much more than a dislike of personal revelation in poetry. It relates to the controversy, still alive in 1874 when the poem was written, concerning the publication of D.G. Rossetti's poems, and, in particular, his sonnet-sequence *The House of Life*. In these very personal sonnets Rossetti revealed much about his relationship with his wife Elizabeth Siddal. Browning's attitude to Rossetti's poetry was equivocal. In "House" he criticizes the inquisitiveness and

prurience of the public, as well as proclaiming that his own poetry
is free from references to his private life. Browning also takes issue
with Wordsworth's view that Shakespeare's sonnets are autobio-
graphical.

Line 4. *Unlock* A reference to Wordsworth's sonnet which begins:
    Scorn not the sonnet; Critic, you have frowned,
    Mindless of its just honours; with this key
    Shakspeare unlocked his heart; the melody
    Of this small lute gave ease to Petrarch's wound ...

35. *dive by the spirit-sense* Must understand intuitively.

How it Strikes a Contemporary
1855 *Men and Women*
    Spain is the setting for Browning's poem about the function of the
poet. The speaker is a Spanish gentleman in 16th-century Madrid
reminiscing about his youth in busy Valladolid. An atmosphere of
suspicion and mistrust, engendered in a superstitious people by the
Spanish Inquisition, is beautifully conveyed when the citizens mistake
the poet for a royal spy. Browning sees the poet as a very ordinary
man, whose special function is to observe scrupulously and to record
accurately. In his *Essay on Shelley* (1851) he had remarked "it is with
this world, as starting point and basis alike, that we shall always have
to concern ourselves: the world is not to be learned and thrown aside,
but reverted to and relearned." The simple events of the poem have
strong allegorical overtones.

Line 3. *Valladolid* City to the north of Madrid, formerly capital of
Spain. Philip II transferred the court and government to Madrid.
Browning read extracts from Lesage's *Gil Blas* when he was at school,
and there came across a Corregidor from Valladolid and also a house-
keeper called Jacinte. It is entirely typical of his method of working
that they should surface thirty years later. Little of his reading was ever
wasted.

6. *courtly once* The beginning of the allegorical side to the poem.

39. *recording chief-inquisitor* Shelley in his *Defence of Poetry* had de-
scribed poets as "the unacknowledged legislators of mankind."

90. *Corregidor* Chief magistrate.

106. *King's work* Soon after the publication of this poem, Brown-
ing wrote to Ruskin, "A poet's affair is with God, to whom he is
accountable, and of whom is his reward."

115. *Prado* The fashionable promenade in the city.

Development
1889 *Asolando*

Browning gives us a rare glimpse into his boyhood. His sister Sarianna claimed that the circumstances described in the poem were real, although the central incident of the "Troy Game" was fanciful. Browning's introduction to Greek, his father's sensible and sympathetic teaching, and the details of his Camberwell home are all authentic. Browning approves of his father's methods of teaching him Greek slowly. From a child's acting-game the boy is gently introduced to Homer in a free and imaginative translation, before being let loose on a Greek text. Having mastered the Greek, he is introduced to Higher Criticism which questions the very existence of Homer and much of the Troy myth. Once Homer can be accepted in this light, Browning is ready for the pure doctrine of Aristotle's *Ethics*. The *Iliad*, taught to him in the way described in the poem, remained one of Browning's favourite books. He possessed a pocket edition which he took with him on his holidays abroad in the 1880's.

Line 1. *My Father* Robert Browning (1782–1866) was indeed a scholar and antiquarian, although he earned his living as a clerk in the Bank of England. He was an unworldly man with a library of over 6,000 volumes which he encouraged Robert to read. Much of the erudition in Browning's poetry can be traced back to the books he read at home. Robert Browning Senior was forced to leave the country in 1852 following a breach of promise case. With his daughter Sarianna he settled in Paris, where he haunted the book-stalls on the banks of the Seine.

11. *the Atreidai* Menelaus and Agamemnon, sons of Atreus.

30. *Pope* Alexander Pope, whose free translation of the *Iliad* in heroic couplets was published in 1720.

43. *Buttmann* Philip Karl Buttmann, German scholar famous for his Greek grammar.

46. *Heine* Christian Heyne published his edition of the *Iliad* in 1802. It was the standard text for many years.

58. *Byron* Lord Byron described Homer as "The blind old man of Scio's rocky isle" in *The Bride of Abydos*, canto 2, stanza 2.

58. *Hymns* ... The hymns to the Gods, the mock-epic *Batrachomyomachia* (*The Battle of the Frogs and Mice*), and a lost work—the humourous *Margites*—were all once attributed to Homer. They are now all accepted as later work.

64. *Wolf* Friedrich Wolf put forward his thesis in the *Prolegomena ad Homerum* that Homer's poems were not the work of one man, but instead were handed down by oral tradition, written down about 550 B.C. and then improved by later writers. These opinions, largely accepted now, caused great controversy. DeVane suggests that Browning, in introducing Wolf as the destroyer of the historical Homer, is drawing an implied parallel with the Higher Biblical Criticism of Strauss and Renan, which in the 1860's attempted to destroy the historical authenticity of the New Testament Gospels.

81. *Spouse* Andromache.

82. *Friend* Patroclus.

100. *Peleus' son* Achilles.

106. *Ethics* Aristotle's *Nicomachean Ethics*.

113. *Stagirite* Aristotle, the Greek philosopher, so called because he was born at Stagira.

Memorabilia
1855 *Men and Women*

No poem better captures the voice and accents of the young Browning than "Memorabilia." His spontaneous enthusiasm and his passionate commitment are shown in this tribute to Shelley's memory. Shelley was Browning's favourite poet as a boy, the dominant influence on his first published book, *Pauline*. The incident described in the poem occurred in Hodgson's, the London bookshop. A stranger entered who, in the course of conversation, spoke of something Shelley had once said to him. Browning's face blanched, and a friend who had accompanied him to the shop laughed at his appearance. Browning explained later to H. Buxton Forman that the "twain became one flesh" in the poem. He told W.G. Kingsland in the 1880's that he still vividly remembered how strongly the presence of a man who had seen and spoken with Shelley affected him.

Title Things worth remembering.

Line 1. *Shelley* Percy Bysshe Shelley (1792–1822), the Romantic poet. Shelley was drowned when Browning was ten years old. Browning discovered Shelley's poetry four or five years later, and found:

> A key to a new world; the muttering
> Of angels, of some thing unguessed by man.

Experience moderated Browning's passion for Shelley's works, but he always admired him as a "subjective" poet. He owned a cast of Marianne Hunt's bust of Shelley (see photograph facing p. 144).

9. *moor* Crossing the moor is one of the metaphorical journeys through life, common in Browning's poetry. The discovery of the eagle's feather relates to the discovery of Shelley's poetry.

The Guardian-Angel
1855 *Men and Women*

The biographical facts relating to this poem are well-established. In July 1848, two years after their marriage, Robert and Elizabeth Browning visited Fano on the Adriatic. In the church of San Agostino they admired Guercino's painting *L'Angelo Custode*, returning to look at it three times. Fano itself proved a disappointment and they moved up the coast to Ancona where Browning wrote the poem. It was one of very few he wrote during the first three years of his marriage, possibly for the reasons mentioned in verse 4. The poem itself is in two parts, the final three verses adding a fresh perspective to the first five, which without them would be sentimental and self-conscious. The introduction of Alfred Domett, Elizabeth and Guercino in the second part changes the direction of the poem. At the end we are left in a very real but imperfect world, in which friends are far away, where painters sometimes paint badly, and where there is much work to do. The cares and new responsibilities Browning was experiencing during his early marriage are clearly evident throughout the poem. In trying to readjust and come to terms with his new life, he writes a poem which effectively demonstrates why he can't write. As such, it is a tour-de-force.

Line 36. *Guercino* Giovanni Francesco Barbieri (1591–1666), known by his nickname Guercino (The Squinter). Browning would have seen his "Woman taken in Adultery" in the Dulwich Picture Gallery when a boy. "The Guardian-Angel" is not a particularly accomplished painting, but it appealed to Browning who had sentimental artistic tastes.

37. *Alfred* Alfred Domett (1811–1887), poet and lawyer, close friend of Browning and with him member of a literary circle, The Colloquials, which met in the 1840's. He left for New Zealand in 1842, where he became Prime Minister, before returning to England in 1872. The subject of Browning's poem "Waring."

46. *My angel* Elizabeth. The sheer inadequacy of this word pinpoints the linguistic problem of the whole poem—and contributes to its greatness.

51. *wrong* Guercino's art was attacked by Ruskin and by Anna Jameson, both of whom were friends of Browning and Elizabeth.

55. *Wairoa* A river in New Zealand.

By The Fire-side
1855 *Men and Women*
The autobiographical "By the Fire-side" depicts a more profound and settled relationship between husband and wife than "The Guardian-Angel." It encompasses past, present and future. The present is a domestic scene in their Florence home, Casa Guidi, with Robert sitting opposite Elizabeth who is reading by the fire. Robert's thoughts move ahead confidently to old age, secure in a deep mutual spiritual love which will, he believes, transcend death. He also looks back to the time when he and Elizabeth recognized the fullness and completeness of their love for each other. Mairi Calcraft has convincingly identified the scene of this recognition as beside the Refubbri Oratorio della Madonna near Bagni di Lucca. It would seem, therefore, that the love which grew in Wimpole Street, and which led to the marriage and flight to Italy in 1846, reached a fuller understanding and confirmation during the summer of 1849, amid the woods and mountains of Bagni. When questioned by a member of the Browning Society about the circumstances of the poem, Browning was characteristically evasive. He acknowledged the emotional truth, but maintained the specific events were imaginary. This contradicts what he had earlier told Mrs. Orr, and should be seen, therefore, as yet another attempt to protect his private life.

Line 18. *branch-work* He daydreams and thinks back to earlier days in Italy.

43. *Pella* Unidentified. There is a Pella on Lake Orta, but, as the scene described is near Bagni di Lucca, this can't be the place. Dr. Calcraft suggests it might be a villa or natural white landmark in an area where white marble is plentiful.

58. *boss* The central ornament on a shield.

64. *freaked* Streaked.

89. *John in the Desert* St. John the Baptist.

92. *pent-house* Projecting awning or canopy.

95. *'Five, six, nine* i.e. 1569.

101. *Leonor* Elizabeth is likened to Leonora, the faithful wife in Beethoven's opera *Fidelio*.

105. *path grey heads abhor* The path to death.

132. *great Word* Death. Cf. Revelation, 21:5: "And he that sat upon the throne said, 'Behold I make all things new.'"

135. *not made with hands* Cf. 2 Corinthians, 5:1.

182. *stock* Tree stump.

185. *chrysolite* Olive-green precious stone. The star is Venus.

229. *shadowy third* The shadow of an ideal relationship that might have been.

241. *How the world . . .* In this stanza Browning points the moral of the poem: the recognition of the "good minute." Cf. "The Statue and the Bust" where it is rejected, and "Two in the Campagna" where it is sought but lost.

255. *One born to love you* James Reeves maintains that this is the clearest statement Browning ever made of his considered view of his own life.

Prospice
1864 *Dramatis Personae*

The death of Elizabeth in June 1861, although not unexpected, temporarily overwhelmed Browning. For a month he stayed on at Casa Guidi settling his affairs, annotating books and manuscripts with poignant comments. In Elizabeth's Bible he wrote a translation from Dante: "Thus I believe, thus I affirm, thus I am certain it is, that from this life I shall pass to another better, there, where that Lady lives of whom my soul was enamoured." Towards the end of this bleak period he sat down to write "Prospice," which, in its confidence of reunion, supports the view of life and death he had expressed earlier in "By the Fire-side." In August he left Florence for ever, taking with him his twelve-year-old son Pen to a new life in London.

Title Look forward.

Line 7. *Arch Fear* Not death itself, but the fear of death.

"O lyric Love"
1868 *The Ring and the Book*

After Elizabeth's death her presence remained with Browning for the twenty-eight long years still left to him, during which he would write over half his poetry. Her memory was the inspiration behind his greatest and most ambitious work *The Ring and the Book*. This poem in four volumes describes a 17th-century Roman murder, and then retells it ten times from different points of view. Before embarking on the first retelling, Browning invokes Elizabeth as his muse in the extract "O lyric Love." This exquisite passage conveys some of Browning's deepest and most personal feelings.

Line 1. *half angel* Compare this with the use of the same word in "The Guardian-Angel."

6. *Yet human* Apart from the surface meaning, this line has a personal significance, a tribute to Elizabeth's first recognition of

Browning's genius as a poet when in "Lady Geraldine's Courtship"
she wrote:

> "Or from Browning some 'Pomegranate,' which, if cut
>   deep down the middle,
> Shows a heart within blood-tinctured, of a veined
>   humanity."

10. *to suffer or to die* The echo of Christ's task in this line is paral-
leled with the Marian salutation in line 12.

Never the Time and the Place
1883 *Jocoseria*

The memory of Elizabeth haunts this lyric written twenty years
after her death. In the delightful springtime Browning is frustrated by
his physical separation from his dead wife. She is in the grave and he
can only approach her in his dreams, but even that is unsatisfactory,
because of a guilt which causes his cheek to flush. This guilt is never
explained, but it can confidently be assumed to be feelings of disloyalty
to Elizabeth's memory. These had first been created in 1869 when
Browning rejected Lady Ashburton's proposal of marriage, and they
had been the emotional source of his long poem *Fifine at the Fair*. In the
present lyric Browning is able to quieten his frustration by projecting
his past happiness with Elizabeth into the future, when he will be
reunited with her after death.

Epilogue
1889 *Asolando*

In the last decade of his life Browning met Katharine Bronson, a rich
American woman who lived with her daughter in a small palazzo (Ca
Alvisi) on the Grand Canal in Venice. Their friendship prospered, and
Browning and his sister spent a number of autumns in Venice with the
Bronsons. In 1885 Mrs. Bronson was widowed. There are suggestions
that Browning contemplated a closer relationship, which was frus-
trated by Mrs. Bronson's inability to understand his feelings. The
poem "Inapprehensiveness" deals with this situation, as does the
"Epilogue" to Browning's final book *Asolando*. In this poem, ad-
dressed to Mrs. Bronson, Browning asks her how she will remember
him when he is dead, and proceeds to give a valedictory assessment of
himself and of his attitude towards life.

Line 6. *mistaken* Mrs. Bronson has failed to understand Brown-
ing's needs. She has worshipped him as a poet rather than loving him
as a man. She has cosseted him.

CHRONOLOGY OF BROWNING'S LIFE

Poems which appear in the anthology and which relate in some way to events in Browning's life are listed beside the chronology. They have not been placed in order of composition or publication.

1812	Born 7 May in Camberwell, London, to Robert and Sarah Anna Wiedemann Browning. His sister Sarianna born 1814.	
1817–26	Educated at a local school in Peckham, which he left at 14. Studied with tutors and in his father's library.	*Development*
ca. 1824	Wrote precocious juvenile poetry which he destroyed. Two poems from this period survived.	
1826	Discovered Shelley's poetry, which influenced him greatly.	*Memorabilia*
1828	Entered the University of London, but withdrew in the following year.	
1833	*Pauline*, his first book, published anonymously. After reading J.S. Mill's criticisms, he tried to withdraw all copies. Twenty-three copies are known to survive.	
1834	Journey to Russia for two months.	*Iuàn Iuànovitch*
1835	*Paracelsus*, his second book, published at his father's expense. Praised by Wordsworth, it established Browning's early reputation.	
1836	Contributed to *The Monthly Repository*.	*Porphyria's Lover*
1837	*Strafford*, his first play, produced at Covent Garden by W.C. Macready, was unsuccessful.	
1838	First Italian journey in search of local colour for his new poem *Sordello*, about the 13th-century Mantuan troubadour mentioned in Dante's *Purgatorio*. Strongly influenced by Venice and the Veneto. Saw Asolo for the first time.	*A Toccata of Galuppi's*
1840	Disastrous reception of *Sordello* (pronounced unreadable) hindered his career for the next twenty years.	

1841–46	Published *Bells and Pomegranates*, eight pamphlets, which include some of his best work: *Pippa Passes* (1841), *Dramatic Lyrics* (1842), *Dramatic Romances and Lyrics* (1845).	*My Last Duchess* "*How they brought the Good News*"
1844	Second Italian journey; visited Rome. In England, first critical assessment of Browning's work appeared in R.H. Horne's *A New Spirit of the Age*. Elizabeth Barrett published *Poems*, in two volumes, which mentions *Bells and Pomegranates*.	*The Bishop orders his Tomb*
1845	Browning wrote to Miss Barrett 10 January and visited her at Wimpole Street on 20 May for the first time. By the end of the year they had fallen in love.	
1846	Married Elizabeth Barrett 12 September without her family's knowledge. Left for Paris, en route to Italy, 19 September. Rented rooms in Pisa 18 October.	
1847	Moved to Florence and settled in Casa Guidi. With Elizabeth explored the city, its art treasures and the surrounding district. By carriage and mule to Vallombrosa.	*Fra Lippo Lippi Andrea del Sarto The Statue and the Bust*
1848	July holiday on Adriatic coast.	*The Guardian-Angel*
1849	Birth of only child, Robert Wiedemann (Pen). Death of Browning's mother. Collected edition of *Poems*, 2 volumes, appeared. First holiday in Bagni di Lucca (June–October).	*By the Fire-side*
1850	Published *Christmas-Eve and Easter-Day*, two poems in which Browning worked out his religious beliefs. Influenced by his marriage and by the death of his mother, it proved to be a commercial and critical failure.	
1851–52	Visited Paris and London.	
1852	"An Essay on Shelley" published by Edward Moxon as an introduction to a volume of Shelley's letters, which proved spurious and was withdrawn. The essay, which contains Browning's views on subjective and objective poets, is one of his few attempts at critical theory.	
1855	*Men and Women*, arguably Browning's greatest single collection of poems, published to a cool critical reception. It includes: "Fra Lippo Lippi," "Andrea del Sarto," "Childe Roland," "Love among the Ruins," "Two in the Campagna" etc.	
1855–56	Visited Paris and London.	*Apparent Failure*

1856	John Kenyon, friend of both Robert and Elizabeth, died—leaving them a legacy of £11,000, which ensured their financial independence.	
1857	Edward Moulton-Barrett, Elizabeth's father, died without accepting the marriage.	
1860	Purchased the Old Yellow Book for one lira from a stall in the square of San Lorenzo in Florence. This was to become the main source for *The Ring and the Book*.	
1861	Elizabeth died at Casa Guidi 29 June.	*Prospice*
1862	Settled with Pen at 19, Warwick Crescent, London. Long summer holiday in Brittany at Pornic.	*Gold Hair*
1864	*Dramatis Personae* achieved limited critical acclaim— and a second edition.	*Confessions* *In the Doorway*
1865	Browning changed publishers, from the lazy and lacklustre Edward and Frederic Chapman to the vigorous George Smith, who became a close friend.	
1866	Browning's father died in Paris.	
1867	Hon. Fellow, Balliol College, Oxford. Hon. M.A., Oxford University.	
1868–69	*The Ring and the Book* published, establishing Browning's reputation.	*"O lyric Love"*
1869	Louisa, Lady Ashburton proposed marriage on holiday at Loch Luichart, Scotland, and was turned down.	
1871	*Balaustion's Adventure*, a retelling of Euripides' *Alcestis*, delighted Browning's readers, just as *Prince Hohenstiel-Schwaungau*, a satire on Napoleon III, puzzled them.	
1872	*Fifine at the Fair*, the product of Browning's French holidays and the Ashburton proposal.	
1873	*Red Cotton Night-cap Country*, a narrative poem dealing with a contemporary scandal in France. It was inspired by a holiday at St. Aubin in Normandy the previous year, and was dedicated to Anne Thackeray, the novelist's daughter.	
1876	*Pacchiarotto*, following *The Inn Album* of the previous year, puzzled even Browning's admirers with its apparently prosaic verse. The extravagant and jingling rhymes were particularly criticized.	*House*
1877	*The Agamemnon*, translated from Aeschylus, is now remembered as "The Browning Version," of Terence Rattigan's popular play.	

1878	*La Saisiaz*, a poem about hopes for immortality, occasioned by the sudden death — in the previous year — of Annie Egerton Smith while at Villa La Saisiaz, Collonges, near Geneva, with Browning and his sister. "Ivàn Ivànovitch," soon to appear in *Dramatic Idyls*, written at Splügen.	
1879–80	*Dramatic Idyls*, first and second series, which saw a return to the dramatic monologues and narrative poems of earlier days. Browning's popularity revived.	*Pan and Luna* *Halbert and Hob*
1881	The Browning Society founded by F.J. Furnivall and Emily Hickey.	
1882	Hon. D.C.L., Oxford University.	
1883	*Jocoseria*, a pot-pourri of short poems, which proved a popular success, thanks to the Browning Society.	*Never the Time and the Place*
1884	*Ferishtah's Fancies*, the first of Browning's retrospective books in which he summarized his ideas. It includes lyrics written to Mrs. Bronson whom he first met in Venice in 1881.	*Ask not one least word of praise*
1887	*Parleyings with Certain People of Importance in Their Day*, Browning's most profound recapitulation of his ideas in autobiographical form. Pen married Fannie Coddington, a wealthy American, and went to live in Venice. Browning left 19 Warwick Crescent for 29 De Vere Gardens. During the move he threw out and burnt many of his personal papers.	
1888–89	*Poetical Works* in 16 volumes, the definitive edition revised by Browning.	
1889	Spent a productive autumn in Asolo preparing his final volume. *Asolando*, dedicated to Mrs. Bronson, published on the day he died, 12 December. His body lay in state in Pen's home, the Ca Rezzonico in Venice, before being taken to the church of San Michele and from there back to England. Buried in Poets' Corner, Westminster Abbey, 31 December.	*Now Inapprehensiveness "Imperante Augusto Natus Est—" Epilogue*